THE

DIALECT AND FOLK-LORE

OF

NORTHAMPTONSHIRE.

BY

THOMAS STERNBERG.

LONDON:

JOHN RUSSELL SMITH, 4, OLD COMPTON ST., SOHO.

NORTHAMPTON :

ABEL AND SONS ; G. N. WETTON.

OUNDLE : R. TODD.—BRACKLEY : A. GREEN.

1851.

PREFACE.

THE following little work is intended to embrace a collection of the lingual localisms; popular superstitions, fairy-lore, and other traces of Teutonic heathenism, to this day preserved among the rural population of Northamptonshire.

The curious dialects of Northamptonshire have hitherto escaped investigation; and with the exception of two short glossaries, appended to the *Village Minstrel*, and *Poems illustrative of Rural Life and Scenery*, of John Clare,* the subjoined collections are now, for the first time, printed.

In the Folk-lore division, it has been thought expedient to confine our notices, for the most part, to the

---

* To these must be added a few words incidentally introduced in Morton's Natural History of the County.

more uncommon and less known of our popular superstitions. The gleanings concerning the fairies will,
probably, be read with interest, as bringing to light
some new particulars concerning this fast disappearing
branch of our popular mythology; and as exemplifying
the elfin creed, not only of Northamptonshire, but
that of the surrounding counties, including Warwickshire, in which most of the legends here given are well
known.

These untutored relations of our peasantry derive
additional claim to our attention when we consider the
possibility of their having amused the infancy of
Shakspeare, and the more than probability that the
vague creations of his rustic neighbours supplied the
foundations upon which were reared the sublime con-
ceptions of a *Midsummer Night's Dream!*

CONTENTS.

PART I.

A

GLOSSARY

OF

NORTHAMPTONSHIRE PROVINCIALISMS.

INTRODUCTORY REMARKS.

THE peasantry of Northamptonshire still retain much of the diversity of dialect which we may suppose to have characterised the early settlers of one of the march or border counties of Mercia and Wessex. Two distinct and very opposite modes of speech may be observed among the rural population of the two extremities of the county. The inhabitants of the districts bordering on Oxford and Buckingham make use of a speech nearly allied to that which is current throughout the Southern and Western counties, and which is generally known as the West Country dialect; while the dwellers in the Northern and Eastern portions of the county speak a variety of the Anglian dialect, more or less similar, according to locality, to those of Leicester, Lincoln, and North Bedford.

In the central districts of Northamptonshire, where the two dialects come into contact, and the Anglian speech of Mercia blends with the Saxon idiom of the West, a third and intermediate variety is current : partaking in some measure of the peculiarities of both, but which, from its utter want of tone, and freedom from dialectic inflexion, has become proverbial among the neighbouring counties for its superior purity and resemblance to our present standard English.   In order to prove that this peculiarity is no result of the various modern causes which militate against the retention of local idiom, we have only to point to the varied and strongly marked dialectic character of the language of the peasantry situated at a greater distance north and south of the Watling Street.*   A passage of Fuller, also, here steps to our aid, and affords a valuable illustration of the point.   In the description of the county prefixed to his list of *Northamptonshire Worthies*, he

---

* Morton has alluded to the supposition that the Watling Street was the boundary between the Mercians and West Saxons, " as it is now the boundary of parishes and lordships, parting betwixt field and field, lordship and lordship, for almost the whole length of its course through the county."—*Natural History of Northamptonshire*, p. 501. This opinion is countenanced in some degree by the language of the peasantry, for the two varieties of which, in the first half of its course, it may be taken as a pretty correct line of demarcation.   The south-western district appears to have been first settled by the men of Wessex ; and in the numerous intestine wars and broils which characterised the days of the Octarchy, it seems, in conjunction with North Oxfordshire, to have constituted a kind of debateable ground between the West Saxons and their powerful Anglian neighbours of Mercia, till finally annexed to Wessex, A. D. 827.

gives the following curious remarks on the dialect:—
" The language of the common people is generally the
best of any shire in England. A proof whereof, when a
boy, I received from a hand-labouring man herein,
which since hath convinced my judgment. ' We speak,
I believe (said he), as good English as any shire in
England, because, though in the singing Psalms some
words are used to make the meeter unknown to us,
yet the last translation of the Bible, which, no doubt,
was done by those learned men in the best English,
agreeth perfectly with the common speech of our
country.' "

It is to this *Lingua franca*, which at the present day
presents precisely the same analogy to the national
speech that the Northamptonshire dialect of the seven-
teenth century did to the language of the Church histo-
rian,—and which is current, in slightly varied forms,
along the whole line of march counties,—that we must,
in all probability, look for the origin of our present literary language. We have, indeed, the authority of Mr.
Guest for looking upon the Leicestershire variety in a
similar light ;* but the *patois* of the Western counties
is no where spoken in that county, and that dialect is
therefore wanting in one of the principal requisites for
the production of a mixed language. To judge, also,
from the printed specimens of Dr. Evans, the speech

* History of English Rhythms. Lond. 1838. Vol. ii. p. 198.

of the Leicestershire peasantry is much more dialectic than the Mercio-Saxon of central Northamptonshire.*

As it will be interesting to the philologist to know how far the Western idiom may have become modified by its proximity to the Anglian dialects, we detail the principal peculiarities of our South-Western district.

The more marked peculiarities of the Western dialect, the interchange of the *v* and *f*, the retention of the *z* sound of the *s*, and the substitution of *d* for the *th*, are all to be observed in this district; though but slightly, in comparison with the usage prevailing in the more Southern provinces. For the long open sound of *a*, or *ai*, in such words as face, bake, fair, &c., the dipthongal sound of *ia* is invariably substituted, making them *fiace, biake*, &c. We, also, still preserve the original sound of the *ea*, thus—break, meat, mean, are pronounced as if written *bre-ak, me-at, me-an*: the pronunciation is perhaps better represented by the insertion of *y*, ·thus—*breyak, meyat*, &c. The dipthongs *oi* and

---

* This view is fully borne out by the Bedfordshire dialect, in which the boundaries of the two varieties appear to be accurately marked by the Ouse; and along the valley of that river we find the same admixture of phraseology, and a similar want of tone. The author of the Herefordshire Glossary (another march county), though apparently unacquainted with the cause, has also a remark strikingly to the purpose:—" It may be observed," he says, " that the Herefordshire dialect is not so remote from the literary language, and does not contain so many provincial expressions as some other local dialect; for example, the Lancashire and Exmoor dialects, as exemplified in *Tim Bobbin*, and the *Exmoor Dialogue*.

oy, as Mr. Jennings has remarked of the Somerset-
shire dialect, and Mr. Akerman of that of Wiltshire,
are commonly changed into *wi*; hence, the usual
spwile for spoil, *bwile* for boil. The long *o* in such
words as boat, coat, lone, &c., receives the sound of *uo*
or *wo*. *Ee* becomes *i*: we continually hear *grin*, *fit*,
wid, *ship*, &c., for green, feet, &c. *Oo* receives the
sound of *u*, as in *bruk*, *tuk*, &c., for brook, took. The
long and broad pronunciation of the *o* in such words as
horn, corn, morning, becomes *a*, thus making *harn*, *carn*,
marnen, &c. ; and the curious form of the verb substantive, *you'm*, *we'm*, *he'm*, we possess in common with
the counties of Bedford and Somerset. The broad
sound of the *ou* in fought, bought, &c., becomes *o*,
rendering them *fote*, *bote*, &c. *D* after *n* is very
generally omitted, as in *groun*, *boun*, for ground,
bound, &c.

The dialects of the Northern and Eastern districts
may be esteemed identical in all essential particulars.
Great diversity of pronunciation is, however, observable
in different localities ; and the speech in general is
much less uniform than that of the inhabitants to the
south of the Watling Street. The pronunciation of a
word will often vary considerably in the same village ;
and numerous changes are apparent in the articulation
of the vowels. The provincialisms of this part of
Northamptonshire, as will be seen from the following
Glossary, betray evident traces of Danish colonization.

Among the distinctive peculiarities of this dialect, as opposed to the rival idiom, we may mention a broader and more open enunciation of the vowels—the substitution of the dipthongal *oi* for the *i* long, in such words as mile, fine, &c., making them *moile*, *foin*, &c.; the substitution of *ai* in the place of the dipthong *ea*; and the preference shown to the plural *are* in place of the legitimate *am* or *be*—"I are, he are," are barbarisms constantly heard. On the borders of Leicester and Rutland the long open sound of the *a*, in such words as day, maid, &c., has a strong tendency to become *e*. The inflexions of the verbs are often omitted, and words in which *a* has the short sound of *o*, as in wash, mash, &c., become *waish*, *maish*, &c.

In the neighbourhood of Thrapstone the speech of the country people is characterised by a very general omission of the article and preposition: a peculiarity which by no means improves the beauty of the phraseology.

According to Mastin, the inhabitants of the Highlands about Naseby were noted for the loudness of their utterance. "They speak a kind of provincial dialect, and in general vociferate very loudly, supposed to be owing to their being brought up in so elevated a situation, where the winds, storms, and tempests, particularly in the winter season, prevail so far as to confound their language." *History of Naseby.* *Camb.* 1792.

Dissimilar as are the methods of pronunciation in

the two districts, the verbal peculiarities are not less so, and are equally suggestive of the diverse origin of the populations. In our progress from North to South, not only do we meet with many striking variations in the verbs and other terms of colloquial intercourse, but the substantives, names of natural objects, birds, plants, &c., undergo a marked and decided change. Many instances of this will be found in the subjoined Glossary. We may point, for instance, to the lady-bird (*Cocinella L.*), which in the Southern district is termed the "lady-lock;" in the *Lingua franca*, " keow-lady ;" and still farther North, the " clock," or "clock-a-clay." The process of collecting corn after the reapers, known in the Southern district as " leasing," is called " picking," or " poikin," in some parts of North Northamptonshire and Leicestershire ; while in the central districts no other term is recognised than the orthodox "gleaning." In the Northern and South-Eastern districts, the words, bridge, shock, must, and self, assume the North-Country form of *brig, stouk, mun,* and *sen.**

The value and utility of provincial glossaries is now

---

* These material differences in our provincialisms render it desirable that each word should, as far as possible, be assigned to its correct limit : in the Glossary, therefore, the *n.* and *s.*, to distinguish our *northern* and *southern* provincialisms, take the place generally assigned to the usual, but somewhat unnecessary, abbreviations of the parts of speech. Their absence, for the most part, implies that the term is common to both dialects.

so fully established, and generally acknowledged, that
any remarks on that head would be superfluous. It
therefore only remains to state the system which has
been pursued in the present collection. Considering
the diverse nature of the Northamptonshire dialects,
it has appeared to the compiler that a complete list of
all the provincial words and phrases used within the
limits of the county would much increase the size of the
volume, without adding an equivalent increase to our
stock of philological knowledge. Under this impression he has omitted numerous words occurring in other
glossaries, such as *stale, law*, &c., which, though perhaps provincial, can scarcely be termed dialectal. Had
he aimed at a complete glossary, he must have inserted
the whole of Batchelor's Bedfordshire Collection,
scarcely a word recorded in which but is also current
in the neighbouring districts of Northamptonshire.
Modern vulgarisms have, in all cases, been omitted ;
and great care has been taken to prevent the admission
of any word not properly indigenous to the county—a
precaution which, in our days of change and locomo-
tion, when the lingual peculiarities of our provinces are
daily becoming modified by the approach of the school-
master and steam-engine, can scarcely be too rigidly
exercised.

THE

NORTHAMPTONSHIRE GLOSSARY.

A. This pronoun, which has the sound of the inarticulate *a*, is used for he, she, and sometimes it; similar to the *ou* described by Marshall, and as having the same force in Gloucestershire. In the northern parts of the county, its signification is generally confined to the first person, masculine. Ancient instances of a similar usage are too common to need quotation here.

2. With. Ex. "a cam in *a* me," she came in with me.

ABEER, *s.* To bear with, tolerate. "I kaint *abeer* him." A. S. *abœran*, tolerare.

ADDLE, *n.* To earn. A. S *œdlean*, præmium. Car. Tees. Ev.

ADDLE, ADLAND } The head-land of a field. Harts. Ev.

AFEAR, *s.* To frighten. "That dwant *afear* ma." A. S. *fœran*. Hart, *fear*.

AFEARD. Pret. of the above. To be found in Chaucer, and most of the early writers. Ak. Her. Bar. Jen. Ev. Hart.

AFIELD. Gone to the fields, out in them. "Wheer's

B

maester?" "Up *afield*." An extension of the principle on which such words as aboard, ajar, &c. are formed.

AFTER-MATH. The second crop of grass. A. S. *æfter post, math* messis. Also called *Latter-math*. Ak.

AGEN. Against. A. S. *agen*. For. Tees. Hart. Bar.

AGGLE, *s*. To cut uneven. A. S. *haccan*. Sui. G. *hagga*, cædere. Ak. *agg*. Car. *haggle*.

AHENT, *n*. Behind. Jam. Ev.

AHOH, *s*. All on one side. "The luoad's all *ahoh*." A. S. *awoh* torte. Ak. Hart. ayoh.

AISTER-EAL. Easter-ale. An extra allowance of ale given to the labourers at Easter, *(pron.* Aister,) as on the other great festivals of the Church.

AIRN, *s*. Either of them, e'er a one. "He have *airn*." Bar. arn.

AKKER, *s*. To shake or tremble. A. S. *acolian*, frigere. Ak.

AKKERD, *s*. Awkward. The full open sound of the *or* and *aw*, is almost unknown in the southern district; thus we have *arched* for orchard, *crass* for cross, &c.

AKKERN, *s*. An acorn. A. S. *akærn*. Dan. *aggern*. Tc. *akarn*. Hart. *akkorn*.

ALM. An elm. Sw. *Alm*.

ALMEN. Made of elm.

AMWAST. Almost. *Amaist* is the northern form. Vide Hart.

AN, *s*. } Of. Invariably so before a vowel. Ex. "I
ON, *n*. } yerd nothin *an* it." Shortened before a consonant to *a*. Ex. "A piece *a* me-at"

ANEEND. On end. "Set it *aneend*." Wilb. Hart.

ANEW, *n.* Enough. The plural form, as some writers call it ; but with us used "promiscuously."

ANNY, *s.* Only.

APPLE, *s.* To bottom or "root" firmly ; spoken of turnips, &c.

> "Unless the soil has some mixture of sand, the turnips do not *apple*, as they call it : that is, do not bottom well."
>
> *Morton*, p. 487.

ARG, *n.* To quarrel. "Them two be ollas *argin*." Not, I am inclined to think, a corruption of *argue*, but the Sw. *arg*, iratus, iracundus.

ARGISOME. Quarrelsome. To which the above derivation may, with more propriety, be assigned.

ARR, *n.* To incite, to quarrel, to egg on. Ben Jonson, in his Grammar, gives the interjection, "*Rr*, that serveth to set dogs by the ears," (ed. 1838, p. 782,) in which sense it is yet far from being obsolete. *Tarre* is used in the same sense in Cheshire. A. S. *terian*, to provoke.

> "*R* is for the dog."
>
> *Shaks. Rom. and Jul.* ii. 4.

ARRA, *s.* ⎫ Either. "*Arra* you or I."
ARR,   ⎬ 2. Ever. "Dye *arra* me-an to dut."
A. S. *æfre*. In the South Northamptonshire dialect the *v* has a strong tendency to go out, when placed between two vowels.

ARRA-ONE, ⎫ Either one. "You may have *arrun*."
ARRUN,   ⎬ Ever-a-one.

ARRA-WIG, *s.* An ear-wig. Germ. *ohrwurm*.

ARRER, *s.* Rather. " I'd *arrer* hav't than all your money ;" i. e. rather have it, &c. A. S. *œr*, prius. Germ. *eher*.

ASCHES, *n.* Ashes. A. S. *asce.* Germ. *ashe.*

AT. To. So used in the phrases, "Wants doin summet *at ;*" " What are ye gwain *at ?*" i. e. to do.

A'TEN, *s.* Often. Jen. *oten.*

ATTER, ⎱ After. Jen. Hart. *attar*. The A. S.
ARTER, ⎰ *œfter*, with the customary elision of the *f*.
   2. Used as a verb. To pursue, follow. " He got the start, but I preshus quick *atter'd* him."

ATNUN, *s.* Afternoon. A. S. *nun*, noon.

ATHIN, *s.* Within. Ak.

ATHIRST, *n.* Thirsty.

ATHISSENS, *n* In this manner. " Do it *athissens.*" In the same strain we have *a'thattens ;* i. e. in that manner. Ev. For. *thissens.*

ATWO. Divided in two. Ak.

AUNTY, *n.* Frisky, spoken of horses, &c. According to Dr. Evans, from "*anticky ;*" i. e. full of anticks.

AX. To ask. A. S. *acksian.* Used provincially throughout England.

BACK-SIDE. The back yard or garden of a house. Ak. Hart. Bar.

> " About this time that untoward generation of Quakers began to bury theirs distinctly by themselves, in their gardens and orchards, in severall places of the towne ; all which burialls (there being no notice given of them to the minister or parish clerke) are here omitted — — — as also

those of several other sort of phanaticks, who
having forsaken the church, woulde not be buried
in the churchyard, but in their orchards or *backside*
of yr houses."

Parish Register of Bugbrook, under 1688.

BADLY, *n.* Sickly. " She looks but *badly.*" Ev.

BAG, *s.* To bag peas, is to cut them with a *hook* or
bill. Wel. *bach,* a hook. Her. Hart.

2. The udder of cows. D. R.

3. The smallest of the titmouse species. It probably receives its name from the peculiar manner in which it forms its nest, bearing a fancied resemblance to a bag. It is sometimes
called the puddin-bag, and in Suffolk has the
name of puddin-poke, which in the phraseology of that county is synonymous.

BALK, *n.* A beam. Dan. *bielke.* Bel. *balk.* For.
Hart.

2. A division or boundary in a field. A. S. *balc.*
Teut. *balck.* In the old Swedish law-books
balk takes the place of capita or chapters.

BALLET, *s.* A ballad. It. *balleta.* The Song of
Solomon (Cantica Canticorum) is styled by old
writers, " The *Ballett* of Ballettes." Very many
old ballads, well worth the collecting, are current
among the peasantry. When tending to illustrate
the meaning of a word, occasional references to them
will be given in the following pages. This promising branch of literary archæology has received but
little attention, so far as the midland counties are
concerned.

BALTER, *s.* A round mass of conglomerated sand; also used as a verb "to *balter.*" In Bedfordshire, according to Batchelor, hasty pudding is said to be "*boltered,*" when much of the flour remains in lumps.

BANG. To move with violence; hence a "*bang-about.*"

BARK. The hard outside of meat.

BARNISH, *n.* To grow fat. "Why ye be got *barn-ish'd* sin yiv bin awey." Ev.

BARM, *s.* Yeast. A. S. *beorma.* Dan. *barm.* This is the common term in the southern district, but in some parts of north Northamptonshire and Bedfordshire, the word is entirely unknown.

BARLEY-BREAD, *s.* An amusement practised by children, similar to the cockle-bread mentioned by Aubrey and Kennet, and quoted in Soane's New Curiosities of Literature, vol. i. p. 199.

BARLEY-BUMP. A contemptuous appellation for a sluggard. The derivation I cannot even guess at, unless it has some connexion with "*bump,*" a term expressive of a dull heavy sound. In Norfolk the bittern is called the "bottle-*bump.*"

BASH, *s.* To beat down fruit, &c. with a pole. Sui. G. *basa,* verberare.

BASTE. To beat. Ic. *beysta.* Fr. *bastonner.* Ak. Hart. &c.

> "I forbodden yeow to meddle with the old carle,
> and let me alone with him, yet yeow still be at him,
> hee serv'-a yeow but weel to *bast* ye for't."
>
> *Late Lancashire Witches,* 1646, i. 1.

BATTEN, *n.* To grow fat. Ev. " to *batten* out,"
also to bask : " Them pigs *batten* in the sun."

BATTER, *n.* To splash with mud. Cla.

BAVER, *s.* The afternoon meal or "drink." The
dramatists, and some dialects, have it *bever.*

BAVIN, *s.* A faggot. Ak. For. Bar. D. R.

BAY, *n.* The space between the main beams of a
barn. For.

BEANT, *s.* Be not. The verb, to be, retains much of
its primitive form in this dialect; instead of I am,
thou art, he is, I be, thou be'st, he be, are constantly heard. In the past tense *wur* takes the
place of was. Us wur, ye wur, them wur, for we
were, &c.

BEAR'S-MUCK. A species of peat, mixed with clay
of very tenacious character.

BEDAG, *n.* To bespatter with moisture. Dan. *bed-
agger.*

BED-EEL, *n.* A species of eel found in the Neu,
as "lying always in clusters or *beds* at the bottom of
the river, until they are roused by violent floods."

Morton.

BEDS, *s.* Anthills.

BEEFER. A familiar name for a calf.

BEGGAR-BANGER, *s.* An officer under the corpo-
ration of Brackley, whose duty it is to "*bang*,"
i. e. expel all beggars from the limits of the town.
The ancient town of Brackley has always been
famous for these gentry. Vide *Proverbs.*

In Cheshire these officials are termed *bang*-beggars.
Wilb. in v. Teut. *bangelin,* percutio.

BELEW, *s.* A disturbance. A. S. *balew*, malus.

BELL, *s.* To make a loud noise, to cry out. A. S. *bellan*, Ic. *belia*. Hart.

BELIKE, *n.* Perhaps. "*Belike* you 'ull," perhaps you will.

BELT, *s.* To beat. Perhaps originally from the implement of chastisement, a *belt* formed like strap, &c. Hart.

2. To clip the tangled locks from sheep. M.

BENCH, *n.* Vide *Post*.

BENTS. The seed-stalks of grass. Teut. *bintz* juncus. Her. Ak. Car. For. Hart.

BETTY, *s.* An instrument used in washing, to fix on a tub in order to let clothes drain through. Probably merely an allusion to the female name, common in like cases; hence, in Shropshire, *Dolly* is the name given to the washing beetle. Hart. in v.

BEWOTTLE, *s.* To confuse or render light-headed. "He's amwust *bewottled* me." Jen. has the *part. bewottled.*

BIDDY, *s.* A word used to call chickens, &c. A. S. *Biddan* to ask or pray. The "coom *biddy*," so often heard in the poultry-yard, is therefore literally, "Come, I bid thee."

BIDE, *s.* To stay or remain. "I bent gwain to *bide* here na langer." A. S. *bidan.* Sw. *bida.* Common to the West country dialect.

2. To endure, synonymous with what in modern parlance we express by stand, "I kent *abide* it," I cannot stand it. The hard kind of free-

stone, which is used for hearth-stones, is said to "*abide* the fire." Vide *Morton*, p. 116.

BILLET, *s.* Wood chopped into convenient shape for burning. Query from *bill?* *Bar.*

> "*Billett* and log-woode to be pilede in large stackes for the house use."
>
> *Order and Government of a Nobleman's House.*
>
> *Arch.* xiii. 375.

BINGE. To soak a bucket, tub, &c., in order to prevent it from leaking.

BIRDER. The wild cat. Morton. "Many years ago, we had wild cats in our Northamptonshire woods, as appears by the charter of king Richard I. to the abbot and convent of Peterborough, giving them leave to hunt the hare, the fox, and the wild cat, which charter was afterwards confirmed by king Richard III. A. D. 1253. And we now meet with them, though more rarely, since the woods have been thinned. These, from their way of living, which is catching birds, &c., on which chiefly they feed, are here called *birders.*" p. 443.

Their loud and discordant wail may still be heard among the lonely lodges and "out" farm-houses, in the vicinage of the forests of Whittlewood and Whittlebury; but the race appears to have degenerated since the days of Morton, probably by admixture with the domestic species.

BIRD-KEEP, *s.* To keep birds from the new-sown corn, by means of "shooing," trumpets, &c. *Bar.* *birdkippy.*

BISHOPED, *s.* Confirmed. A. S. *biscopod*, confirmatus. In the same manner we have "parsoned," married. Hart. For.

BISNINGS, } The first milk yielded by the cow
BEESTINGS, } after calving. Ev. *beestings.* For. *beastlings.* Hart. *beestings.* Bat. A. S. *bysting.*

BIST, *s.* Art. " Thee *bist.*" A. S. *bist.* Ak. Hart.

BITTERSWEET, *s.* The woody nightshade. Gerarde.

BLACK PARR, *s.* In order to frighten children into good behaviour they tell them here that *Black Parr* will have them. Who this gentleman is or was, they appear to have lost all account. Probably he was a member of the family of Parr, Marquis of Northampton, who was nearly allied to the Greens of Greens Norton. We find from Baker that two members of this family served the office of sheriff in the reign of Henry VIII. Must we not ascribe the bug-bear celebrity to one of these gentlemen?

BLARIN, *s.* Loud talking. Dut. *blaren*, to make a loud noise.

BLAST, *n.* The blight.

BLATHER. A bladder. Ak. We have also *lather* for ladder, *ether* for adder.

BLAW, *s.* To cry loud. Wel. *blaw*, clamor.

BLEAK, *n.* Pale, sickly looking. A. S. *blœce.* For. Ev.

BLIZZEY, *s.* A blaze. A. S. *blysa* fax. Ak.

BLOACHED, *n.* Blotched, or presenting a variegated appearance, as the " *bloached* holly."

BLOBS. A name given to several large flowers. Water-lilies are called " water-*blobs.*"

2. Drops or globules of water. Hart.

BLOW, *s.* A bud or blossom. Wel. *bloen.* Ak. *blowings.*

BOBBIN JOAN, *s.* The arum. Also the name of an old country dance, not yet forgotten in this district. In the " Complete Country Dancing Master," we find it under the name of " *Bobbin Joe.*"

BOBBISH. Lively, brisk. Ex. " How bist 'e ?" " Purty *bobbish,* thankee." Ak. Will. in *bobber.* Hart. Forby derives it from the Old Fr. *bobe,* a joke.

BOD. To take off the husks of walnuts. A Wiltshire word. Ak.

BODY-HORSE. The second horse in a team. Her. Bat.

BOG, *s.* To move off, to budge. Fr. *bouger.* Germ. *bewegen.* There is also the Ic. *bog,* a leg or limb, from the verb *bagen,* flectere.

BOLT-HOLE. The hole from which the rabbit makes its escape; or, in the phraseology of the craft, " *bolts.*"

BOOSING, *n.* The trough or manger in a cow-house. A. S. *bosig.* M. Ev. *booson.* Her. *boosy.* Tees. *buse.* Hart. *boosey.*

BOOT. " A kind of punishment to such boys as have carelessly neglected their duty in the harvest, or treated their labour with negligence instead of attention, as letting their cattle get pounded, or overthrowing their loads, &c. A long form is placed in the kitchen, upon which the boys who have worked well sit, as a terror and disgrace to the rest, in a bent posture, with their hands laid on each other's backs, forming a hedge for the " hogs," as the truant boys are called, to pass over ; while a strong chap stands on each side with a boot-legging, soundly strapping them as they scuffle over the bridge, which is done as fast as their ingenuity can carry them."

> *Clare's Village Minstrel,* p. **xxiii.**

This forms a good comment upon the passage in the Two Gentlemen of Verona, act i. sc. 1.

BOSKY. Intoxicated. Devonshire.

BOSS, *s.* A round large stone or iron ball, used in marble playing.

2. To bowl with a *boss.* Germ. *bosseln,* to bowl.

BOTE, *s.* Bought. Jen.

BOTTLE, *s.* A bundle of hay or straw. In Barret's Dictionary, 1580, it is rendered " Fasiculus vel manipulus sæni."

> " Marry sir, I am seeking a needle in a *bottle* of hay, a monster in the likeness of a man : one that, instead of good-morrow, asketh what porridge you have for dinner."
>
> *Haughton's Englishman for my Money,* 1598. i. 2.
>
> " This I am sure, a needle may be sooner found in a *bottle* of hay, (a task though difficult, yet possible to be done,) than the arms of some sheriffs of counties to be found in the herald's visitation of the said counties."
>
> *Fuller's Worthies,* 1682, p. 49.

BOULDER. A name applied to any large round stone. In Wiltshire they give it to the large insulated stones found on the downs. The word is now, I believe, a recognised term of geological nomenclature.

BRACKLE, *n.* Brittle.

2. To break into many small fragments, as is customary with loamy soils. Morton. A. S. *brecan*, frangere.

BRAKE. A field after the corn has been reaped.

BRATTLINGS, *n.* Loppings from felled trees. For.

BRAVE, *s.* Hearty, in good health. " Old Gaffer's lookin quite *brave*."

BRAWN, *n.* A boar pig. Ev. For. Hart.

> " Sir Thomas Androwes, a worshipfull knighte of Northamptonshire, was by a yeomanly man, his neyghbour, thoughte to be sometime too much affectioned to the matter he liked well, to whom he broughte a greate *brawne*: the servant letting hys maister, the knyghte, understand of thys present, retourned him to knowe the givers name, which hearing, he could not call to remembraunce any suche, but *forthe* he comes : The presenter doth hys errand, prayes his maistership to take in good part this poore pigge, and with very lowe cursey wishes it better. Sir Thomas saw the swyne was good with mustarde, accepted the gift, demanding his neyghbour why hee was at that coste with hym, sith he neither knew him, nor ever had done hym any pleasure. ' There it is' (quoth he, with a long leg in his hose) ; ' neither will I require you to do me any : but I bestowe this hog on your worship that you shall do me no harm.' "
>
> *Arthur Hall's Works*, (about 1579) rep. 1814.

BRENT, *n.* The brow of a hill. Ev. Sw. G. *bryn*, vertex montis. Sw. *brunt*, abruptus.

BRIG, *n.* A bridge. A. S. *brycg.* Common to all the Northern dialects.

BRIEF, *n.* Common, prevalent, " Colds are *brief*." Ev. Bar. Hart.

BREVIT. To hunt, rummage. " *Brevitin* about." Ak. Ev. Hart. *brevet.*

BROCK. A badger. Morton Ev. A. S. *broc.*

BUCK, *s.* To wash, rain, perspire, on wet in any way: hence showery weather is called " *bucking* weather." A person heated by running or violent exercise is said to be " *bucked.*" Goth. *bucka,* lavere. Germ. *beuchen.* A. S. *byken,* macerare, lixivio.

BUCK-TUB. A large round tub used in washing. A. S. *buc,* interpreted by Somner, " a vessel for the purpose of washing, like a hollow semicircle." We have also *buck*-basket, as the designation of a washing utensil, exactly similar to the one into which we may suppose Falstaff to have been betrayed :—*Merry Wives of Windsor,* Act III., sc. 5.

BUCK-WASH. A large wash, *i. e.* one in which the large " buck-tubs" are used : a " *buck*" of clothes, in its common acceptation, means as much as can be contained in one of the large baskets.

> " But now, of late not able to travel with her furred pack, she washes *bucks* here at home."
>
> *2nd Henry VI.,* iv. 2.

BULL'D. Swollen. Dan. *bullen.* Shakspeare has *boll'n* in the same sense, Rape of Lucrece. Sw. *bula,* protuberantia.

BULLOSIN, *s.* " Gwain *bullosin,*" *i. e.* gathering the bullace, or wild damson.

BUM, *n.* To rush with a heavy murmuring sound. Teut. *Bommen,* sonare.

BUMBAL, *s.* A clot of cow-dung.

BUMMING, *n.* The humming noise made by insects :

hence the humble-bee retains with us its primitive designation of *bumble*-bee (Beaumont and Fletcher, iv. 72).

BUMPTIOUS. Overbearing, arrogant. Ev.

BUN. That part of the bean-stalks which is left by the scythe after mowing—*i. e.* the stubble. Batch. Dan. *bund.* Gael. *bun*, bottom or foundation.

BUNG, *s.* A term for a sharp, lively fellow. Shakspeare would seem to imply by it a person of a different character.

> "Away, you cut-purse rascal, you filthy *bung*, away!"
>
> *2 Henry IV.* ii. 4.

BUNJELL. A hard blow.

BUNT. The smut in corn. Perhaps a corruption of *burnt*. Grose gives this as a Northamptonshire provincialism.

2. To assist in climbing with the head. " *Bunt* me up." "Gie me a *bunt*." Ak. Harts.

3. The common puff-ball, a species of fungi.

BURNT-TO, *n.* In boiling milk or porridge, if care be not taken, it sometimes encrusts the pan and acquires a nauseous taste, it is then said to be *burnt-to.*

> " If the podech be *burned-to,* or the meate overroasted, we saye the Byshope hath put his fote in the potte; or the Byshope hath played the coke : because the Byshopes burn who they lust, and whosoever displeaseth them."
>
> *Tyndale's " Obedyence of a Chrysten Man,"* 4to. 1528.

BURR, BURROW, *s.* The shade. "The *burr* side of the hedge." Mr. Akerman gives as the etymon the A. S. *burh*, which he says originally meant a place of shelter. Ak. Herf. (Gl.)

BURR, *s.* A sharp blow.

2. The sweet-bread of a calf.   Herf. Harts.

BUTTY, *n.* A companion or partner.   Ev. Herf. Harts.   The author of the Herefordshire Glossary considers it a corruption of *abettor.*   Mr: Hartshorne gives the A. S. *Bote,* auxilium.

BUTTON, *n.* A small mushroom, a fungus.   Harts.

BUTTRY, *s.* The pantry of a cottage or farm-house. Fr. *bouter,* a pantry.   Ak. Bar.

BUZZARD. The cockchafer: most likely so called from the buzzing sound attendant upon its flight. Harts. *Blind-buzzard.*

CAC, *s.* Stercus.   CACHUS latrina.   A. S. *cac cachus.*

CADGER. A beggar.   Ev.   In Cheshire they give this term to a carrier.   Wilb. in *v.* Broc, a packman.

CAFFLE, *n.* To quarrel.   Probably a corruption of *cavil.*

CAG, *n.* To crawl, move slowly.   Ev.

CALLICE. Sand of a large grit.

CANK. Punishment.

CANKER. A small caterpillar.

2. A sore place, frequently occuring on the lips of men and cattle; perhaps deriving its name from the above, as it is often erroneously supposed to be caused by one of those insects.

> "*Canker* is in his mouth venomed, and will make his tongue to have cliftes, and scabbes in his upper lippes underneath, and are full of blacke wheales or pimples, so that he can hardly eat his meate."
>
> "*A very Perfect Discourse ; how to Know the Age of a Horse,*" &c.   Lond. 1610.

CAP, *n.* The top sheaf of a shock. Wel. *cap*, a covering.

2. To excel or outdo. Ex. "That *caps* him all to nothing." For.

CAR, *s.* To carry. pron. *kyar.* Bar.

CART, *n.* The harvest-home festival.

CASS'NT, *s.* Canst not. A Western peculiarity. Ak.

CAST. The second swarm of bees from the hive. In the old writers we find the word "*cast*" used to express a couple; hence Beaumont and Fletcher—

> "Yonder's a *cast* of coach mares of the gentlewoman's, the strongest cattle!"
>
> *Scornful Lady,* Act ii. Sc. 2.

This would appear to have some connexion with the meaning in the present instance. Mr. Hartshorne, in the Shropshire Glossary appended to his Salopia Antiqua, gives as the probable etymology, Sw. *kast*, abjicere. Ic. *kast*, missio. Hart. Bat.

CAT-CORNER'D, *s.* A corruption of cater-cornered. *Vide* Ev. Bat. in *v.*

CATE, *n.* A cake. "As the words *make* and *mate* were in some cases used promiscuously by ancient writers, so the words *cake* and *cate* seem to have been applied with the same indifferency: this will illustrate that common English proverb—"To turn *cat* in pan" (*i. e. cate*). A pancake is in Northamptonshire still called a "*pancate*." Gloss. to Vol. i. of Percy's Reliques. Hence we have also *chisket*, a cheese-cake.

CAUSEY, *n.* A causeway. Dut. *kautsije.* Lanc. Bat.

c

CAVINS. The ears of corn after the grain has been threshed out. A. S. *ceaf*. Germ. *kaf* palea.

CHAPMANRY, CHAPMONEY. Allowance money made by the seller to the buyer after payment. This word is now almost obsolete, having merged into the modern "discount." M. A. S. *ceapean*, to bargain.

CHAPS. The fissures into which the land is broken after a long continuance of hot weather.

CHAR, *s.* A job, or short piece of work. A *chare-woman* is a female who goes out to work by the day. Also used as a verb. To *char*, *char'd*, &c.

"That *char* is *char'd*, as the good wife said when she had hanged her husband."

Old Proverb, cited by Ray.

"I have neay time now up the town to rume, There is odd *charrs* for me to deau at hame."

Praise of Yorkshire Ale, 1697.

CHARM. To make a noise or clamour. A. S. *cyrm*, a noise. Ak. Bar. Hart.

CHATS, *n.* Small sticks used for burning. Ev. Hart.

CHATTER, *s.* The peculiar sound made by the hen before she sits: also applied to the chirp of the sparrow. Dut. *citteren*, tremere.

CHAW, *s.* To chew with disgust. In Bedfordshire, according to Bat. "*chou.*" A. S. *Ceowan*, ruminare.

CHERRY-CURDS. The first milk from the cow after calving.

CHIMBLE, *n.* To crumble into small fragments: hence, also, to gnaw as a mouse. Ev.

CHIMBLY. A chimney. Ak. Car. For. &c.

CHINK, *s.* A fool.

CHIP, *s.* Cheap.

CHIT, *s.* To bud or germinate. A. S. *cit.* Ak.

    2. A shoot or tender stalk; or the first sprout of
corn from the seed. Bat.

CHITLIN. The name of a small and early kind of
apple.

CHITTERLINGS. The entrails of a pig. Belg.
schyterlingh. Car. Tees. Ak.

CHIVVY, *n.* A chase. Forby derives it from " an
obvious allusion to the national ballad !"

CHIZZELLY. A term applied to that species of land
which breaks when it is turned up by the plough
into bits, in size like the chips that are usually made
by the chisel of the stone-cutter. Morton.

CHOCK, *s.* A blow. Old Fr. *choc,* a shock, &c.

CHUMBLED, *n.* Pret. of *to chimble.*

> " Where hips and haws for food suffice,
> That *chumbled* lie about his hole."
> *Clare's Shepherd's Calendar,* p. 31.

CHUMP. A log of wood for burning. For. Tees.

CLACK. Talk, gossipping conversation. Teut. *klack,*
sonora percussio.

CLAM'D, *n.* Exhausted from want of food. Willan.
Car. Wilb. in *clem.* Ev. Moor. For. Herf. Teut.
Belg. *klemmen,* stringere. Dan. *klemme.* Dirt or
clay adhering to a spade is said to *clam.* Dut. *klam.*

CLANE. Clean: also pronounced *clen.* A. S. *clane*
and *clæn.* Besides its usual acceptation, used in the

sense of completely, entirely: thus—"*clane* gone ;"
" *clan* tuck-to."

> " Being seated, and domestic broils
> Clean overblown."
>
>   *Shakespeare.*

> " I found my good bow *clene* cast on one side."
>   *Ascham's Toxophilus*, p. 7. 1544.

CLANE, } *n.* The after-birth of a cow or sheep.
CLE-AN, } Lanc. *cleaoning.* Ev *clans.* Car.
        } Tees. *cleaning.* Bat. *klian.*

CLAT, *s.* To congeal or coagulate.

2. A clod or lump of any substance ; hence " cow-
clat," " earth-*clat*." Ak. Teut. *klotte.* A. S.
clat, gleba.

CLATTER BANGIN, *s.* A compound word to express
violent motion attended with noise.

CLAUM, *s.* To seize or handle roughly. A. S. *clu-
mian*, to press. Ak. *clum.*

CLEEKIN, *s.* The impression of horses' hoofs upon
soft ground. Teut. *kaucken*, calcare. Hartshorne
has " *corking*, the turned up bits on the toe of a
horseshoe "

CLEFT, *s.* A log of fire-wood ; one that has been cleft
from the trunk.

CLEVER-THROUGH, *n.* Strait through. Ex.
" You must go *clever-through* Stanford." More a
Leicestershire phrase than a Northamptonshire one.
Ev.

CLICK, *s.* A sharp blow. " A geunne me zich a
klick a th' yead." Dut. *klick.*

CLICKER, *s.* The cutter out in a shoe-making establishment. In the " Dictionary of the Terms, Ancient and Modern, of the Canting Crew," Lond. n. d. (but prior to 1700), he is described as "the shoemaker's journeyman, or servant, that cutts out all the work, and stands at or walks before the door, and saies— what d'ye lack, sir? what d'ye buy, madam ?"

CLIP. To stick or adhere to. A. S. *cleopan.*

2. To run or walk fast: "*clip* along." Germ. *kleppen.*

3. A method by which boys determine the choice of sides, adjust differences, &c. Vide Moor in *v.*

CLIT, *s.* To cleave tightly together. Wel. *clyttian.*

CLOCK-A-CLAY. The lady-bird. (*coccinella* L.) Germ. *chuleich,* scarabæus. Jam. *clock-bee,* a species of beetle.

CLOD-HOPPER, *n.* The weat-ear or fallow smicht : according to Morton, so called from its clod-hopping propensities.

CLOMBER, *s.* Intensitive of to climb.

CLOMPER. To walk or tread heavily, so as to produce a loud sound. Car. in *clamp.* For. Belg. *klomper.* Teut. *klumpern,* metallum tundere.

CLOUGH. A large, shallow earthen pan. Morton.

CLUMP, *n.* A bulky mass. The Triticum spica multiplica, or many-eared wheat, is called *clump*-ear'd wheat, from its bulk. Sw. *klimp.*

CLUMPY, *n.* Bulky. "A *clumpy* fellow."

CLUNCH, *n.* A hard kind of peat, found mixed with sand, &c. Germ. *klunt,* massa concreta.

CLYTEN, *s.* Pale, sickly. Mr. Akerman (Wiltshire

Glossary) defines it " An unhealthy appearance, especially in children."

COCK, *s.* The top of a rick, stack, &c.   Celt. *cok*, caput.

COD,   } *s.* To cover, or wrap up. A. S. *cod*, a
CODDLE, }   cover or husk.

CODDY-MODDY, *n.* According to Morton, a species of sea-gull, flocking to the Northamptonshire lowlands, in great numbers, during the autumn and winter months.

CODGEL, *s.* To manage, or do easily. " I'll *codgel* it somehow."   Ev. *codge* in a similar sense.

COLCH. To fall in or give way, as the sides of a gravel pit. Wel. *cau.* Germ. *caw*, cavus. In Norfolk, to *cave.* Harts. *cave.* Ev. *carved* in.

COLT. The third swarm of bees.   In order to express the comparative value of each swarm, our rustics have the following rhyme. A Warwickshire version, very similar, is given in Hone's Every-Day Book.

> " A swarm of bees in May
> . Be worth a load a hay ;
> A swarm in June
> Be worth a silver spune (spoon) ;
> A swarm in July
> Bent worth a fly."

COLT, *s.* To give a man the freedom of a new place, &c., after having treated his new comrades to an allowance of ale. The ceremony consists in holding up his leg and striking the sole of his foot with a board. Bar. For. Moor. Bat.

COMMINS, *n.* Commonage. " The right of *commins*."

CONEY-GREE. Frequently the name of a rabbit-warren. Hart.

> "Parkis, Warrens et *connigries*."
>
> *Stat.* 13, *Rich. II.* c. 13.

' In Barret's Dictionary (Lond. 1580) Park is rendered "anie place enclosed to keepe beasts for pleasure : a *connigree*, a warraine."

CONKER, *n.* A cucumber. Fr. *concombre.*

COOP, *n.* To throw.

COPSE, *s.* A moveable frame-work attached to the common carts in the carriage of hay or corn. Bat.

COPWEB, *n.* A small bird, which makes its nest in the corners of walls, where spiders weave their webs. Morton.

CORD, *n.* A stack of wood : a stated quantity or measure, varying in different districts. M.

COSTERPENCE, *s.* Morton informs us that the country people about Wardon call the old Roman coins which are frequently found there *costerpence,* corruptly, he thinks, for *caster-pence.*

COTTER, *n.* To plague or contend with. Ev. Teut. *koter-én,* fodicare.

COUNT, *s.* To suppose or reckon. Perhaps the pronunciation would be better conveyed by *key-ount.* Bat. Bar.

CRAIN, *n.* A species of wild ranunculus, bearing bright yellow flowers.

CRAMP. The noise made by swine in eating. Hart. *crump.*

CRAMP-BONE. The *patella* of a sheep or lamb, worn about the person as an amulet, to keep off cramp.

One instance of a human *patella* being thus used has come under my notice, but I believe such instances to be by no means common.

CRAKER. A turncoat, one who confesses. Belg. *kraecken*, gloriari.

> " Pitty the Braggar, the *Craker* will take care on hissen."
> *Northamptonshire Proverb.*

CRANE, *n.* A game which frequently enlivens the proceedings of the harvest-home feast.

> " A man holds in his hands a long stick, with another tied to the top of it, in the form of an L reversed, which represents the long neck and beak of the crane. This, with himself, is entirely covered with a large sheet. He mostly makes excellent sport, as he puts the whole company to the rout, pecking at the young girls and old men's heads; nor stands he upon the least ceremony in this character, but takes the liberty to break the master's pipe, and spills his beer, as freely as those of his men. This mostly begins the night's diversions, as the prologue to the rest; while the booted hogs wind up the entertainment."
> *Clare. Introduc. to Village Minstrel,* p. xxii.

CRANK, *n.* To sing dolefully, to croak. In the Glossary to Tim Bobbin, *crank* is rendered, " The noise made by a raven, also to prate."

> " ——— the solitary crane
> Swings lonely to unfrozen dykes again,
> *Cranking* a jarring melancholy cry."
> *Shep. Cal.* p. 31.

CRANKY, *a.* Unsound : applied as well to furniture, &c., as to human beings. The word appears to be the same with the *cranky* of the Prompt. Parv. Dut. *crank.* Germ. *krank,* sickly, feeble, &c. . In the old dramatists, and some of the northern dialects, it is used to express the reverse,—*i. e.* sprightly and lively. Howell, in the Introduction to his " Lexicon Tetraglotten," 1660, remarks, " Some critics observe that the English language takes the liberty to alter sometimes the sense of the words which she borrows ; as she useth *crank* for being lively and well, whereas 'tis sick in Dutch," &c. Ev. has *crank*, sick.

CRASH. *See* Creach.

CRATCH, *n.* A rack for holding hay. M. Hart. Ev. Moor. Her. Fr. *creieche.*

CRAW, *s.* The bosom. The old shirt-buckles which adorned our ancestors of the last century, and even till late years, in our secluded districts, were usually called *craw*-buckles.

CRAWIN, *s.* " Gwain *crawin*," *i. e.* catching the cray or craw fish, which abound in many of the Northamptonshire brooks.

CREACH, *n.* The thin lamina of the limestone. Morton, p. 41.

CREACHY-LAND, *n.* Soil strewn with the above. Morton.

CREEMY, *n* Trembling, nervous.

CREENY, *s.* Small, diminutive. Ak.

CRICKS, *n.* Dry and narrow perpendicular fissures in stone strata Morton, p. 123.

CRINKLIN, *s.* A small early apple. In Herf. a " *crick*" is a very small child. Harts.

CRIZZLE, *n.* To freeze. So used by Clare.

CROCK, *s.* A pot or pan. A. S. *crocca.* Ak.

CROCUS-MEN, *s.* The managers of an old ceremonial custom, in the liberty of Warkworth, were formerly so designated. *Vide* Bridges' History of Northamptonshire, vol. i. p. 219. Brand, vol. ii. pp. 12, 13.

CROFT. A small field near a house; often found connected with some other word, as corn-*croft*, hay-*croft*, &c.

CROODLE, *n.* To crouch or shrink. For.

> " And *croodling* shepherds bend along,
> Crouching to the whizzing storms."
>
> *Shep. Cal.* p. 26.

CROP, *n.* A species of kealy limestone. Morton, p. 104.

2. A stock or bed of quarry stone.

> " Were there any sure indications of stone : could there be given, I mean, any certain rules or directions where to find a shock or *crop*, as the stone-diggers call it, of useful quarry-stone," &c.
>
> *Morton*, p. 118.

CROSS-HILL. The open space in the centre of a village, otherwise called the green, in the middle of which is frequently to be found the assemblage of rude steps, still known by the name of the cross, though the iconoclasm of the puritanical times has rarely, if ever, allowed its more distinguishing characteristic to remain. Forming, as it were, the nucleus of the village, it is the most frequented resort of the idlers and holiday makers. Around its base are practised the sports of May-day, and the feast, at which time it was customary to decorate the shafts with boughs, flowers, &c. In some villages it appears to have been applied to a more useful purpose. · The shaft of the cross at Irthingborough was, in the time

of Bridges, " used as a standard for the pole to measure out their parts or doles in the meadows." Vol.
ii. p. 235.

CROSS-MONDAY. The Monday after the festival of
the Invention of the Cross. Old style, May 14th.

CROW-FARLINS. *i. e.* crow-fallings. Small twigs
and pieces of branches broken off by the crows.

CRUEL, *s.* Excessive, " *cruel* bad." Palmer's Devonshire Glossary. We have also in the same sense,
" deadly," " gallus," &c.

CRUP. *Pret.* of to creep. A. S. *creopan*, to creep.

CUBBY-HOLE, *s.* A snug place. Ak. Bar.

CUCKOO-LAMB, *s.* A lamb born about April, the
time of the cuckoo's first appearance.

CUE, *s.* A cow's shoe. Her. Ak. Bar.

CALLINGS, *n.* Refuse corn, &c.

CUMBERGROUNDS, *n.* A name for useless trees.
Clare.

> " Cut it down, why cumbereth it the ground."

CUNNINGMAN, *s.* A conjuror, or discoverer of
stolen goods. A branch of imposture now pretty
well extinct.

CURL, *n.* A species of marcasite. Morton.

CUT-MEAT, *n.* Oat-straw, &c., reduced to chaff for
fodder. M.

DAB, *s.* To throw or slam with force. Dan. *dabe,* a
faving beetle. Bat. has " *dob,* to throw with gentle
force."

DABSTER, *s.* A proficient. Ak. Jen. Bat. Bar.

DABWASH. A small wash, in contradistinction to a buck-wash, *q. v.* For. *slop-wash.*

DAD, *s.* Father. *Vide* Shaks. King John II. sc. 2. Arthur Hall (Works, p. 109) calls Cicero " the *dad* of the Romayne eloquence." There is a ludicrous saying, illustrative of the progressive refinement in food and language.

> " Dad, mam, and porridge ;
> Father, mother, and broth ;
> Pa, ma, and soup."

DAG, *s.* A sharp sudden pain. Bat.

DAGGERS, *s.* Icicles. A. S. *daag,* anything hanging. Wiltshire *daglets.* Ak.

DAGLOCKS. *s.* Dirty flakes of wool on sheep. A. S. *deagan,* to dirty. Ic. *deiga,* madefacere.

DALE-MIST. A valley, or lowland mist. Morton, p. 336.

DAMPS, DAMPERS, { *n.* Fissures intersecting strata : those that are filled with earthy matter only are called damps.

DANCE, *n.* A convulsive disorder incidental to swine : so called because, as Morton informs us (p. 454), " they shake and quake in every part. They change their postures so often, that they resemble the actors in a Morris dance."

DANE'S-MONEY, *s.* All old coins that are found in the earth are so designated by our rustics. To the same source they ascribe the origin of most of the ancient remains ; and innumerable legends are still current of battles, burnings, &c., in which the Danes play the most conspicuous part. There would appear

still to remain a traditional remembrance of their
oppression.

DANG'T, *s.* A contraction of *God-hang it.* " *Dang't,*
Bill, dwant say so."

DAPS, *s.* The very *daps* of him—*i. e.* the very likeness. Bar.

DARE, *n.* To frighten. " Don't *dare* that child." Dan.
daarer, to make mad. Wel. *dera*, insania furor.

> "——— which drawne, a crimson dew
> Fell from his bosome on the earth : the wound did
> *dare* him so."
>
> *Chapman's Homer*, xi.

DEADLY, *s.* Very, exceedingly. Ex. " *deadly* gret,"
" *deadly* merry," very merry. On the same principle we have " tearing big," " pestilent fine," &c.
" Nation big," commonly supposed to be a contraction of a more expressive word."

DEA-NETTLE. The wild hemp plant. M.

DECK, *n.* A pack of cards. Shaks. Wilb. Hart.

DECK. To desert or break an engagement on some
frivolous pretence. Ex. " I'll *deck* the job." Dan.
dækkerr, a blind pretence or colouring.

DELF. An old stone or gravel pit. Teut. *delve*, fovea.
Hart.

DELVE, *n.* To dig. A. S. *delfan.* Dut. *delvan.*
Tees. Hart.

DEVIL'S FINGER RING. The large hairy caterpillar.

DEWK, ⎧ To bend or stoop. " That tree *dewks.*" Bat.
DOUK. ⎨ Hart. Belg. *duyk-en*, to stoop. Sui
       ⎩ G. *duka*, deprimere.

DIDS, *s.* Breasts, or paps.

DING, *n.* To taunt or reprove. "*Ding'd* on the nouse." Teut. *dinghen,* contendere.

2. A blow; from which, most probably, the preceding word is derived. For. Hart. Sui G. *dænge,* tundere.

DINNY, *s.* To make a noise. "Dwant *dinny* me." We are informed in the " Clavis" appended to "The Praise of Yorkshire Ale," 1697, that " *Din* is noyse." A. S. *dynan,* sonare.

DITCH, *n.* To stick or adhere, as mud to the spade. Ev.

DITHER. To tremble. Wilb. Ev. Hunter's Hallamshire Glossary. Lond. 1829.

DOB, DOBBIN, — *s.* A term for a foolish fellow; also the usual contraction for Robert. Carew, in his survey of Cornwall (1602), describing the dialect of the Cornish, says—" James they call Immey; Walter, Watty; Robert, *Dobby,* &c."

DOD, DODDER. — An aquatic plant. The village of Dodford, in this county, is supposed to derive its name from the abundance of it found there. Fuller—Worthies of Northamptonshire, p. 290, 1662— speaking of Dodford, says, "So named, I take it, from a ford over the river Avon; and *dods,* water-weeds (commonly called by children cats' tails), growing thereabouts."

DOLE, *s.* To toll. An interchange of the *t* and *d*, common to the Western dialect.

2. A share or allotment in the common field; still retained in the names of fields when applied to fields near a river: it may, perhaps, be derived from the Wel. *dol.*

DOLLOP. A lump or large piece. Ev.

DON, *s.* To do on. In the same manner we have *doff*, to do off. Jen. Car. Bar. Broc.

DON, *n.* Clever, expert. " He's a *don* hand at shootin."

DONNER, *n.* Anything well performed is said to be a *donner.*

DONKEY, } *n.* Wet, moist, or damp: generally ap-
DONK, } plied to land. M. Dut. *donker*, obscure. Germ. *tuncken*, damp. Sui G. *dunken*, mucidus.

DOODLIN, *s.* Lingering. " What are ye *doodlin* for ?"

DOOMOT, *s.* A merry-making, or feast. A. S. *dom*, council; *mot*, an assembly. In Frisian and old German, *dom* is the common term for a house or dwelling. Car. has the word " *do*," a fete.

DOSSITY, *s.* Life or spirit.

> " She sat herself down soon as got in the house,
> No *dossity* in her to stir."
>
> *Clare's Vill. Min.* p. 156.

Among Batchelor's Distortions, we find it written "*dositi*," and rendered " sharpness." In Leicestershire, according to Dr. Evans, it signifies " ailing, infirm."

DOTTERIL, *s.* An old tree; one that has lost its " head," as the woodmen phrase it.

DOUGH-KIVVER. The chest or trough in which the dough is made.

DOUT, *s.* To do out, to extinguish. Ak. Her. Bar. Hart.

> "I have a speech of fire, that fain would blaze,
> But that this folly *douts* it."
>
> *Hamlet*, iv. 7.

DOWSE, *s.* A blow. Ak.

DRAP-DUMPLINGS. Dumplings compounded of flour and water. *Vide* Moor, in drop-dumplings.

DRESSIN, *i. e.* dressing. Separating corn from the chaff. Bat.

DRIBBLINS. The last drops from the cow at a milking. For. *strippings.* Har. *drippings.* A. S. *dreopan,* stellare.

DROPPLE. To rain in large drops, as in a storm.

DROUTH, *s.* Thirst. Ak. Jen. Bar.

DROWK, *n.* Drooping: Clare's Vil. Min. p. 46.

DROWN, *n.* To inundate. Land under water is said to be drowned. Thus the Nea annually *drowns* the meadows near its banks. One of the fen-men's objections to the Earl of Lindsey's project was—

> "That the fens in question were not *drowned,* and did, therefore, need no draining." (No. 6.)

And thus Ben Johnson, in the "Sad Shepherd,"

> "Down to the *drowned* lands of Lincolnshire."

DROWNINGS, *n.* Fens, of which the eastern districts of the county formerly chiefly consisted. Their state is thus described by an old writer :—

> "The aer nebulous, grosse, and full of harres; the water putred and muddy—yea, full of loathsome

vermene ; the earth spaing, vafast, and boggie; the fire noysome, turfe and lassocks— such are the inconuiniences of the *drownings*."

A Discorvse concerning the Drayning of Fennes.
Lond. 1629. 4to.

DUBBY, *s.* Blunt. Ak. Bar. Ic. *dubba*, percutere.

DUCK-SHOWER. A shower of short continuance.

DUDMAN, *n.* A scare-crow. Qy. Whether a corruption of the Herefordshire *dead-man* or *dud-man*, *i. e.* a man of rags?

DUFHUS, *s.* A pigeon-house. For. A. S. Sw. *dufhus.*

DULL. Deaf.

DUMMIL, *n.* Heavy, stupid. Ev.

DUSTY-MILLER, *n.* A kind of rude farce performed at the harvest supper. *Vide Clare's Vil. Min.* xxiv.

DUDDER, }
DUTHER, } *s.* To confuse. A. S. *dyderian.*

DWIZY, *s.* Sleepy. Dan. *dvals*, a dead sleep.

DWIZEND, *s.* Deadlike, having a withered appearance. A. S. *dwinan.* Belg. *dwynen*, languere. Bat.

" A *dowzand* leauke is a withered look."
Clavis to Yorkshire Ale. Lond. 1697.

EALD, *s.* To yield. "Apples *eald* well this year."

EALT, *n.* *Pret.* of to ail. "Dunna kneow what *ealt* him."

EANE. To bring forth: applied to an ewe. A. S. Hart. *yean.*

EANIN-TIDE, *s.* The lambing season.

EARTH-QUAKES, *s.* *Briza media*, or quaker-grass.

D

EAY, *n.* A pond or pool; also a drain or artificial water-course. For. A. S. *ea*, aqua.

EDGE, *s.* To move slowly, or by degrees. Ev. Wilb.

EDGY, *n.* Eager. Ev.

EEKLE, *s.* The woodpecker. This bird may be said to be the countryman's barometer: when dead, he hangs it up by the legs, and judges of the weather by the state of its tongue; before rain it expands so much that it protrudes from the mouth, while in mild weather it remains shrivelled up in the head. Ak. *yuckel.* A. S. *wigol fugelas*, oscines aves.

EEL-POUT. The barbot. According to Morton, the Nen is the only Northamptonshire river in which this fish is caught.

EEL-DRIVING. Eel-spearing.

EEND, *n.* End. "The t'other *eend* on't." The use of this word is common to all the Anglian dialects.

EES,
EEZ, } *s.* Yes. A. S. *Gyse:* which, according to Mr. Akerman (Wilt. Gloss.), "must have had the exact sound of this word, the *g* being but slightly sounded, or perhaps not sounded at all."

EES-SURE, *s.* The common form of the positive affirmation.

EGG-ON. To incite to quarrel. Com. Dan. *eggen.* A. S. *eggian.* C.

EKE, *n.* To increase or augment. Harts.

"Then *ekes* his speed, and faces it again."

Shep. Cal. p. 91.

Used in the same sense by Chaucer and other ancient writers. A. S. *eacen.* Ic. *eyk*, augere.

ELDERN, *s.* An elder tree. Ak. Bar.

2. Made of elder. "*Eldern* wine."

ELDIN, *s.* Growing aged. "Gaffer Snelson is som *eldin*," i. e. getting old. A. S. *ealdian.* Dan. *alder*, to grow aged.

ELT. To become soft or moist, as earth when damp. In Lancashire, "to stir dirt;" dough sometimes after kneading. Car. has "*elt*, to knead." "*Elting*-moulds, the soft ridges of new ploughed land." *Gloss. to Clare.*

EMMOT. A lively person. An "*emmet;*" no bad simile.

ETH, *s.* A rabbit earth; also pronounced "*yeth*," the Western word for earth.

ETHER, ⎰ *s.* A hedge, and the radlings of which it is
EDDER, ⎱ composed. A. S. *eder* and *ether.* Hart. *ethering.* Ak. Wilb.

ETTLES, *s.* Nettles.

EVVERN, *s.* Untidy, as regards apparel. Bat.

EYAMS, *s.* In most glossaries *hames.* Pieces of wood attached to the collar of a cart-horse. Ak. Jer. Car. Teut. *hamme*, numella.

FAGGET. A reproachful epithet applied to a female. Her. For. Hart.

FARDEL, *s.* A quantity of valueless articles : this is one acceptation of the word that Shakespeare and other old writers use in the general sense of a pack or burden. It. *fardella.*

> "Which they scrope, and scratch, and patch to-
> gether, like shreds in a beggar's cloake, to make up
> a *fardle* of fooleries, and a bundle of bables."
>
> *The Strange Witch of Greenwich.* Lond. 1650, p. 2.

FARM, *s.* To clean out. "Them housen want well *farmin.*" Common to the Western dialects.

FARRANTLY, *n.* Respectable : "a *farrantly* body." When applied to animals it means strong, vigorous. Ic. *faer,* validus. Ev. Wilb. Hart. Car. *farrendly.*

FAT, *n.* Land is said to be *fat* when subject to mildews.

FATHEN. The wild orache. Car. Tees. Ev.

FAY, *n.* To cleanse or purify : applied to the removing filth from drains, &c. ; synonymous with farm. Ic. *faegia.* Sui. G. *feia,* purgare. Wilb. Ev. Moor. For. in *fie.*

FEED. To fatten. M.

FELT. The fieldfare.

FELTH, *n.* Feeling, "He's lost his *felth.*" Ev. in *feelth.*

FERRICK, *s.* To scratch.

FETTLE, *n.* To settle, arrange, put in order.

    2. Condition. The word in both acceptations is to be found in all the Northern and Midland glossaries.

FEW. A small quantity. "A *few* broth or porridge." Car. Ev. Tees. For.

FEX, *n.* A petty oath : contraction, probably, of I *facks,* or I *fegs.*

FEZZLE, *n.* A litter of pigs. A. S. *faesl.* Ev.

FIG-SUNDAY, *s.* Palm Sunday.

FILBERDS, *s.* Filberts. The old form of the word.

FILLER, } *s.* The shaft-horse; also pronounced
THILLER, }   "*thiller.*" Herf. For.

> "Thou hast got more hair on thy chin than my *thill-horse,* Dobbin, has on his tail."
>
> *Shaks. Mercht. of Venice,* ii. 2.

FILL-DIKE, *n.* The month of February.

> " January white,
> February *fill-dike*."

Old Prov.

FILLIP. To strike with a sudden spring or motion. This word is sometimes used to express a cruel operation on a toad or hedgehog, to which animals it is well known rustics have a great antipathy. Moor. For. in *v.* Willan. in *spang-hew.*

FINCH-BACK. A cow having a white back is said to be *finch*-backed. M.

FIN-WEED, *s.* Rest harrow, the herb so called.

FIRK, *n.* A state of restlessness. " Don't be in such a *firk.*" Sui. G. *fika,* cursitare. Also used as a verb, to fidget. Ev. in *v.*

FISTLES, *n.* Thistles. Bat. Ev. Many other words also exhibit the interchange between the *f* and *th :* thus we have thurrough for furrow, freten for threaten, folentive for volentive, &c.

FIT, *n.* Fought. Ev.

FLACK, *s.* A smart blow with the open hand. For.

FLACKIN-COMB. A wide-toothed comb : this word, and the phrase, " a *flacking* big one," appears to have some connection with the Dan. *flakken,* rambling, &c.

FLAGGY, *s.* Large and thick ; spoken of corn when it approaches the bulk of " flags," or rushes.

FLAZE, *n.* A smoky flame. In Leic. to " *flaze* is to ignite into flame."

FLEAK, *n.* A wattled hurdle. Her. Car. Ev. Germ. *flechte.*

FLIG'D. Fledged. Ic. *fleegar*. Wilb. Tees. Ev. Car.
Hence *fligger*, a young bird just fledged.

FLIT, *s.* To *flit* a hen is to tie it to a stake, so that it
cannot desert its chickens.

FLITTING, *n.* A removing or departing. Dan. *flyter*,
migrare. Wilb. Hart. Car. Bat.

FLOBBER, *s.* Loose, flabby. Teut. *flabbe*.

FOG, *n.* Rank and coarse after-grass. Lanc. Car.
Tees. Ev. For. Moor. Her. *feg*.

FOOTY, *s.* Valueless, paltry. Fr. *foutre*. For. in
foutry. Ak.

FORREST, *s.* First, quasi *fore-est*. The first horse
of a team.

FOT. *Pret.* of the verb to fetch.

FRECKS, *s.* Painful sores appearing at the ends of
the fingers.

FREE-MARTIN. When a cow has two calves at a
birth, male and female, the female, who is generally
barren, goes by the above name. Morton. Car.

FREM, Juicy and succulent : applied chiefly to green
food. Ic. *framar*, mollis. A. S. *from*, strong, stout.

> " But notwithstanding the coldness of the clayey
> soil, it is ordinarily the *fremmest*, as our farmers
> express it ; that is, the richest feeding land we have."
>
> *Morton*, p. 51.

Ak. in *fram*. Wilb. Car. Bat.

FRESH, *n.* This word used in reference to cattle signifies fat, or " well to do." Her.

FREZ, *s.* Furze. The transposition of vowel and
consonant. See *wapse*.

FRIDDLE, To idle or trifle away time.

FRIDGE, *n.* To chafe by friction. Ev. It. *fregare*, friare.

FRIT. *Pret.* of to frighten. " He was som *frit*, warnt he ?"

FRUM. Fine, handsome ; a "*frum* fellow." Hert. A. S. *frum*, principium.

FROUSTY, *s.* Filthy. Swift has *frowzy*.

FULL-SKIT, *s.* At full speed. " He war gwain along at *full-skit*." A. S. *scyte*, in præcipiti. Ic. *skiotr*, celer.

FULL-SWOP. To drop "*full-swop*," *i. e.* with a sudden fall : the same idea is also conveyed by "*flump*" *balsh*, fabricated, probably, from sound. A. S. *swapa*, ruina.

FURRIDGE, *s.* To search or hunt.

FOOT-BRIG, *n.* A plank or trunk of a tree laid over a stream, so as to afford a passage to pedestrians only : thus Clare—

> " Down lane, and close o'er *foot-brig*, gate, and stile."
> *Shep. Cal.* p. 32.

FUZZEN, *s.* Furze.

GAFFER, *s.* A title of respect given to the old ; also used in the sense of master, or headman.

GAIT, *n.* A gait of water is two bucketfuls. In the more southern districts called a *yoke*, from the instrument with which it is carried. By no means peculiar to this county, but common to all the Eastern and Northern dialects.

GALLS, *n.* Wet and moist patches of land. Car. For. Belg. *gouw*, aquagium.

GAMMER, *s.* A respectful title for an old woman.

GAP-HUL, *s.* Gap-hole, a chasm in the earth. Sw. *gapa.*

GAP-MOUTHED, *n.* Having an empty mouth, *i. e.* without teeth.

GARE, *s.* To express surprise by the looks, to stare. A cockney who visited the country was said to go "*garin* about ;" perhaps this remark might be better applied to a countryman's visit to London.

GATTARDS. "Will you go with me *gattards* ?" *i. e.* Will you accompany me on my way home? Dr. Evans, in his "Leicestershire Words," explains this to mean "*gate-wards*," *i. e.* towards the gate ; but it is more probably, as in the Craven dialect, "*gait-wards*," to accompany ; "to gang in the same *gait.*" Car. in *v.*

GAULT, *n.* A blue calcareous clay. For.
2. The bubbling motion produced in a liquid by its rapid conversion into vapour, ebullition.

GEARS. The harness and trappings of horses, &c. Ak. For. Her. A. S. *geara*, apparatus ; also used as a verb, "*Gear* the horses."

GEARING, *s.* The railings round a waggon. M.

GEDD, *n.* A disease in sheep, attended by *giddiness*, from which the name is derived. Ev.

GEUNNE. *Pret.* of to give, or *gie*, as it is here pronounced.

GIE. To give. Common, with slight variations, to all the English and Scotch dialects.

GIFTS. White spots on the finger-nails, indicative, it is believed, of good fortune. Car. Hunter, For. Tees. Bar.

GIG. An old machine for winnowing corn; now grown quite into disuse, being superseded by more recent inventions.

GIMEL, `
GEMEL-TREE. } Two trees of the same species, growing united, trunk to trunk. This is given as a Northamptonshire word by Morton. A *gimmal* ring was a double or twisted one, given by lovers to their mistresses. Jimmers, in the North country dialect, are "jointed hinges." Most etymologists agree in deriving this word from the Latin *gemellus;* it would also appear to be nearly allied to the Dan. *gemal*, a consort, male or female.

GIVE, *s.* To relax, from the dampness of the atmosphere or fermentation, applied to corn. A tub is also said to give when it leaks. Sw. *giften*, leaky; or more probably used in the Norfolk sense of "*forgive*, to begin to thaw." For. in *v.*

GLEG, *n.* A glance. " I geynne a *gleg* at him."

GLENT, *s. Pret.* of to *gline, i. e.* to glance or stare.

GLINK, *n.* The sound which a liquid makes in escaping from a narrow-mouthed vessel. Dan. *glunk.*

GLOWER, *n.* To stare. Jam.

GLUT, *n.* A long continuance of wet weather.

GODDLE, *s.* To deceive. " I ben't agwain to be

goddled a'ter that fashion." Wel. *godwyllaw*, *god-wyll*, a slight deception.

GODLINS. " By *godlins*." Can this be a corruption of " God's limbs," or is it merely an instance of the diminution often found in popular forms of asseveration?

GOLDING, *n.* The corn marigold. Morton. Wilb. Dut. *goudt-bloem*.

GOLLOP, *s.* To swallow greedily. Dut. *golpen*.

GOOD, *n.* Used as a verb. " It wont *good* me none." Pal.

GOODJERS, GOOD-YEAR. { An exclamation of wonder and surprise. " What the *goodjers* be that ?"

" What the *good-year*, my lord ! why are you thus out of measure sad ?"
              Much ado about Nothing, Act. i. sc. 3.

Stevens explains this *gonjeres*, morbus gallicus; but Mr. Collier contends that it is *good-year*, and strengthens his supposition by quotations from cotemporary writers. *Vide Collier's Shaks.* Vol. ii. p. 198. It appears to be but a variation of the common exclamation " *good dear.*"

GOR, *n.* Dirt. A. S. Sw. *gor*. Wilb. For. in *gors*.

GORM, *n.* To dirty. In some parts of the county transposed to *grom*. Her.

GOSSUK, *n.* A bill-hook for cutting goss or furze. Ev.

GOUT, GOAT, { *n.* A ditch or drain. Belg. *gouw*. Flem. *goot*. Fr. *égout*, a drain, &c. Ic. *geota*, caverni terra ; *gut*, foramen. Car.

GOTTY, GOUTY, *n.* Wet and boggy. "A *gouty* field." A piece of land intersected with many small streams, &c., would be called a "*gotty* piece." In Cheshire, *gusout.* Wilb. in *v.*

GRAB, *n.* A grasp. Dan. *grab.*

GRAIN, *n.* The larger branch of a tree. M. Car. Tees. Hart. Dan. *gren.* Ic. *grein.*

GRAINS, *s.* Malt after the water has been pressed through it. Ic. *grion.* Hart.

GRAMMERD, *s.* Grained, as the pores of the skin, with dirt. "How *grammerd* your feayce be."

GRAN-CAP, *s.* A conical covering for the head, made by children of rushes.

GRAVEL, *n.* A ford. In former times it was usual in the fenny districts to fill the beds of rivers and watercourses with gravel, in order to save the expense of building a bridge, which, as it gradually wore away, was supplied with fresh materials by common day-work, at the expense of the parish in which it was situated. Hence the term *gravel*, as applied to a fordable passage, now almost obsolete.

GRET. Familiar, intimate. A. S. *gretan*, to greet. "They two be very *gret*." Found in both the Western and Northern dialects.

GRET. To work by the piece, in contradistinction to time-labour. Ev. Bat.

GRIME, *n.* To blacken. Car. Tees.

GRIP. A narrow ditch or furrow. Car. Her. Jen. Pal. A. S. *grep.*

GROM, *s.* A forked stick used in thatching. Ak.

GRUBBY, *s.* Dirty.

GRUDGINGS. A kind of bran, next to pollard in fineness. Bar. "*gurgeons,* pollard, coarse flour." Ev. Fr. "*escourgeon,* a kind of base and degenerate wheat, which being ground yields very white, but very light, and little nourishing meal." *Howell's Dict.* 1673.

GRUMPY, *n.* Stiff and hard, spoken of soil; and used figuratively for "*saucy,*" ill-tempered. Ev.

GULF-JOINT, *n.* A chasm intersecting strata. Morton, p. 97.

GULLS, GULLEYS. {
Wide and deep fissures, often found intersecting a stratum of stone. Morton. Differing from "*cricks,*" "*seams,*" &c., in being generally filled with earthy matter. The same words are also used to express a drain or small stream. The chasms formed by rooting up trees are also termed "*gull-*hole."
}

"Theyre passage sodeyneley stopped by a greate *gul* (ingens vorago) made with the violence of the streames yt ranne downe the mountaines, by wearing awaye of the earthe."

Brande's Quintus Curtius, fol. 115. 1561.

Allied to the Fr. *goulet.* Sui. G. *goël,* vorago.

GULLED, *n.* Intersected with *gulls.* Thus Clare—

"Close by the rut*gulled* waggon road."

Rural Muse, p. 76.

GULSH, *s.* To tear up with violence, as a stream when swollen with floods.

2. To swallow voraciously. Jen. Teut. *gulsign.*
Germ. *gaufen.*

GUMSH, GUMPTION. { Common sense, understanding. Ak.
Bar. Bat. For. Hart. Jen. Wilb.
in *gawm.* Car. has *gaum,* to
know, to distinguish. Teut.
gaume, acutus. Mœs. G. *gaumian,*
percipere.

GUSTER, *n.* " To be in a *guster,*" *i. e.* out of breath,
in a puffing state. Dan. *gust,* flatus.

GUTTLING, *n.* A *guttling* fellow, a great eater. C.

GUZZLE, GUDJIL, } *s.* A drain. Ak. Bar. Germ. *guss.*

2. Small beer. "Poor *guzzle.*" C.

GWAIN, *s.* Sometimes used in the sense of "to go :"
" Will you *gwain* wi' me ?" but oftener as the *part.*
A. S. *gan.* Germ. *gehen.*

GWAIN-ON, *s.* Going on. Scolding. " He's allas a
gwain on at me."

HATCHLIN, HACKLIN. { The process of turning the hay into
hackles or *hatchels.* Sw. *hackla,*
pectere.

HAG. To fatigue. " I be *hagged* a'moast to death."
" A *haggey* road," one that is tiring to the horses.
Ev. *hagging.*

HAIN, *s.* To preserve a field for mowing, by excluding
cattle from it. Ak. Jen. Bar. Sui. G. *haegn,* a tueri
circumdata sepi. Germ. *hagen,* conservare. Jam.
Broc. to preserve.

HALLON-TIDE. The season of the festival of All

Saints. Before the days of agricultural improvement the operations of the farmer were chiefly regulated by the red letter days. From Michaelmas to *Hallon-tide* was the old rule for the period of sowing wheat.

HALM. Stubble; straw used in thatching. Dan. *halm.* Com.

HAND-PAT, *s.* Ready at, fluent.

HAND'S-CHARE. A slight job, one that requires only a small portion of labour. Ev.

HANDY, *s.* Near to. Ak. Her. Tees. Jen. Bar.
  2. Ready, quick, &c. Hart. A. S. *handlunga,* præsto : "look *handy.*"

HANTLE, *n.* A handful : evidently a corruption.
  2. A scuffle, or scolding bout. Ev.

HAP-LUCK. At hazard, without premeditation. " He did it *hap-luck.*"

> "He is resolved hit-miss, or *happe-go-luck* (according to the country Teutonick), to have a blow at their Jack."
>
> *Vindication of the Conversations of the Town.*
> Lond. 1673.

HAR. To have. A. S. *ah.*

HARD-A-HEARIN. Deaf.

HARDS, *n.* A term applied in the fenny districts to those patches of land which, from superior elevation, or other causes, remain *hard* and dry during the winter season; oases, as it were, upon the dreary expanse of marshes. Before "the drayning of the fennes," the dwellers upon these *hards* were oftentimes exposed to the most distressing privations. An old writer, describing the fens of this and adjoining

counties, thus remarks :—" In winter, when the ice
is strong enough to hinder the passage of boats, and
yet not able to beare a man, the inhabitants upon
the *hards* and the bankes within the fennes, can have
no help of food—no comfort for body or soule—no
woman ayd in her travell—no means to baptize a
child, or to administer the communion—no supply
of any necessitie, saving what these desolate places
can afford."— *Discorse concerning the Drayning of
Fennes*, 1629.

HARVEST-MAN, *s.* The Harry long-legs *(Phalan-
giam opilio)*: one of those insects which superstition protects from wanton injury. Their abundance
is supposed to denote a dry harvest.

HASSACK, *n.* A coarse species of grass, growing in
damp places. The term *hassock*, as applied to foot-
cushions, may possibly be traced to this source. For.
Ev. Sw. *hwass*, juncus.

HAT, *s.* Hot. A. S. *hæta.*

HASKY, *n.* Hard and rough. A person affected with
a severe scorbutic affection described her face as
" very *hasky*." Dr. Evans renders it dry and harsh.
Jam. *hask.*

HASTENER. A screen for the purpose of *hastening*
the cooking of meat.

HAW,
HAY,
{ *s.* A small wood or coppice, used in conjunction with some other word. Swine-
haw, west-*haw*, &c. Germ. *hai.* Sui.
G. *scog.* A. S. *haga*, agellus : nearly
allied to the Northern *shaw*, a wood.
For. in *hag.* Hart. in *hagg.*

HAZZLE, *s.* The appearance presented by the skin before it chaps. A. S. *haswe*, lividus.

HEAD, *n.* Kind or sort. "If their seed be all of one *head*, as they call it, that is, of one particular sort, it sells the better, by sixpence or a shilling a bushel, for seed." *Morton*, p. 477. The A. S. *had*, Sw. *het*, signifies quality, condition.

HEAD-ACHE, *s.* The common corn-poppy, so named from the cephalalgic tendency of the scent. For.

"Called *head-ache* from their sickly smell."
Clare's Shep. Cal. p. 47.

HEAD-AND-ABED. A stone-digger's phrase: a stone is said to rise with a *head-and-abed*, i. e. with an even side and surface. Morton, p. 108.

HEARTH, *n.* The floor on which wood is charred, or the pile of sticks used by charcoal burners for the same purpose. Morton.

HECTH, *s.* Height. Ak.

HEDGE-CHAT, *n.* The common hedge-sparrow.

HEFT, *s.* Weight. "What's th' *heft* on't?" Ak. Jen. Her. Bar. A. S. *hebban*, levare.

HEIT, *n.* A word addressed to the second horse in a team, as a command to turn to the "out"-side of the driver. Mr. Hartshorne derives it from the Persian *heita*, come hither. Used by Chaucer, *Frere's Tale*, Ty. vol. i. p. 287.

HELL-WEED, *s.* A troublesome species of bind-weed (convolvulus arvensis and cascuta). Evidently from the A. S. *helan*, togere.

HEN-MOULD, *n.* A black spongy and mouldering earth, so called, Morton thinks, from its being of that species which poultry take delight to flutter and dust themselves in. p. 37.

HEN-TOED. A person who walks with his feet turned in is said to be *hen-toed.*

HEP, *s.* A heap; also a quantity of persons or things, in which sense it occurs in Layamon. The A. S. *heap*, turma. For. Car.

> " Well said, old honest buddles. Here's a *heap*
> Of merry lasses."
>> *Houghton's Englishman for my Money.*
>> 1578. iii. 3.

> " His frynd sind engla *heapas.*"
>> *Homilies of Ælfric,* Vol. i. p. 340.

HERN-SHAW, *n.* The heron. In the northern part of the county it is known by no other name.

> " Minerva's *hernshaw* and her owl."
>> *B. and F. Masque of Augurs.*

HETTER. Ill-natured, spiteful. "He's allas been uncommon *hetter* agin me." Ev. Ic. *heipta,* animo violento agere. Car. gives "*hotterin,* boiling with passion." Germ. *haderen.*

HEY. To hie. "*Hey* an wi 'e." Ic. *heya.* Dan. *hej,* quickly.

HIDGE, *s.* To walk fast, or with increased speed, as to "*hidge* along." A. S. *higian,* to hasten. We have also the phrase, " to *higg* off," *i. e.* move away quickly. Germ. *hagga*-aff, abscindere (*Lex. Suev. Germ. Lat.* 1640).

HIGH-LARNT, *i. e.* high-learned. A man, wishing to apologise for his ignorance, said he had not been " *high-larnt.*"

E

HIGH-LOWS. Shoes coming up the ancle. For.

HIKE, *s.* To remove anything from its proper place, as " them tots be al *hiked* aff;" also to *hike* off, to decamp hastily. Ak. Jen. Tu. For. Ic. *hika*, cedere. For. *pike*-off.

HIKE, HOICK, $\left\{ \begin{array}{l} n. \text{ To toss at, to gore. Car. M. Hart. Ev.} \\ \text{Her. } hile. \text{ Wilb. } hoyk. \text{ Tees. } hipe. \\ \text{Jen. } hoke. \text{ Bar. } hook. \end{array} \right.$

HILLING, *s.* Bedclothes, or any species of covering. A. S. *helan*, tegere. Pal. has " *hylling*, a covering." Hart. Wilb. Lanc. &c. Jen. gives the West county verb, " *heel*, to hide," and the proverb, " The *heeler* is as bad as the stealer," *i. e.* the receiver is as bad as the thief.

> " Lord, whanne sighen we thee hungry, and we fedden thee? thirsty, and we gaven thee drynke? And whanne sighen we thee herborles, and we her- boreden thee! or nakid, and we *hiliden* thee!"
>
> *Wicliffe, Matthew*, c. 25.

HIND-EEND, *s.* The latter end. " Autumn is the *hind-eend* of the year." Tees. in *hinderend*.

HING, *n.* To hang; so used by Chaucer. " *Hing* sig- nifies hang."— *Yorkshire Ale*, 1697. Car. Hun. Tees.

HIRPLE, *n.* To walk lamely, to limp.

HITHER. Nearest : used in designating fields, as the *hither* delf, wung, &c., meaning the nearest to the homestead.

HOB'S HOG. " You thought wrong, like *Hob's hog*," who, saith tradition, imagined he was going to receive his breakfast when the butcher came to his sty to kill him. Ev.

HOCKSY, *s.* To move or clatter with the feet, " to go *hocksin* about ;" and the phrase to a person in the way, of " *hocksy*," equivalent to move off. Fr. *hocher.* Teut. *hutsen*, to jog.

HODGE, *s.* To patch or sew clumsily.

HODS, *n.* Pieces of turf cut into a quadrel shape. Morton.

HOG-A-WE, *s.* A boyish pastime, in which the chief feature is kicking, or gently striking ; perhaps from the Ic. *hogga*, verberare.

HOGS, *n.* Yearling sheep. Ray gives this as a Northamptonshire word, 1674; used also, he says, in Yorkshire, but now understood to be used in most of the agricultural and grazing counties. N. Fr. *hogetz.* Hart. *hogget.* Jen. Car. Bar. We have the proverb, " to lose a *hog* for a hap'orth o' tar," implying a sarcasm upon niggardly husbandry.

> " Let's not loase an *hogg* for a hawporth of tar."
> *Yorkshire*, p. 42.

> " To conclude with the old proverbe, hee that will loose a sheepe (or a *hogge*) for a pennyworth of tarre, cannot deserve the name of a good husband : you may guesse at my meaning. Honest countrymen, worthy gentlemen, farewell."
> *The Countryman's Instructor.* Lond. 1636.

HOH, } An elevated site : a frequent name for a field
HOO. } in such situations. A. S. *hoh.*

> " *Hoo* is a determination of many places in this shire, as Thornhoo, Cogenhoo, and many others; and it commonly appeareth to be a craggie, rockye, stonye, and thornye place. Barren for the most, and not as profitable as other places."
> *Nordon's Northamptonshire*, 1610. p. 17.

HOLD, *s.* "How d'ye *hold*?" How do you do?" the common form of salutation, meaning, how do you *hold* or retain your health. Ex.

HOLT, *n.* A common name for a field. The A. S. *holt* may, perhaps, admit of a wider signification than wood or grove.

> "Have ye any pigs, calves, or colts;
> Have ye any lambs in your *holts*?"
> *B. and H. Beggar's Bush,* iii. 1.

2. Hold. "Ony let me get *holt* an ye."

3. A quarrel or dispute. Ev.

HOMOCKS, *s.* Large feet and legs. Bat.

HOMOCKIN, *s.* Making a noise with the legs.

HOOD, *s.* Wood.

HOODIN, *s.* Gathering sticks for fuel. "Gwain *hoodin,*" going wooding.

HOOK, *s.* A piece of land situated on a slope.

HOOLET, *n.* An owl. Herf. Car. *hullet.* Tees. *hewlet.*

HOOPIT, *s.* The signal in the children's game of tig: thus, to "cry *hoopit*" is to exercise the lungs pretty lustily. A. S. *hweopan.* Sui. G. *opa,* clamare.

HOPPLES, *n.* Straps for the legs of horses; to "*hopple*" a horse is to fasten his legs with these straps. Ev. Car.

HORSE-THYME. Wild thyme. The prefix added on the same principle as in "*horse-radish,*" "*horse-rennet,*" &c.; similar to the Greek *boo.*

HOT, Did hit. *Pret.* of the verb *hit.* "A *hot* me on my yead."

HOTCHEL, *n.* To move with a hobbling motion.

"It's as much as I can do to *hotchel* along." Belg.
hotten. Jam. *hotch.* Car. *hotch.*

HOUSEN, *s.* Plural of house. Ak. Ev. Jen.

HOUGIN, *s.* A covering attached to a horse's collar.
Wel. *hws.* Fr. *housse.* Hart. Bat.

HOW,
HOO-E, { *n.* A pig and bird propelling imperative.
Ic. *hoa,* greges convocare vel agere.
Moor gives *hoo-e* as a Suffolkism, in
the same sense, "pronounced in a
deep guttural tone." Also a Kentish
provincialism. *Lewis's History of
Tenet.* Lond. 1723. p. 16.

HOWK, *n.* To draw out; "*howk* it out." Dau.
harcken. Teut. *hawcken,* screare. Sui. G. *holka,*
cavare.

HOWP, *n. Pret.* of to help. Bat.

HUB, *n.* The nave of a wheel. M. Bat.

HUBS, *n.* Large rugged stones that will not . stand
frost. Morton.

HUG-MUG, *n.* Confusion, "all in a *hug-mug.*" Shaks.
has *hugger-mugger.*—*Hamlet,* iv. sc. 5.

HULK, *n.* A temporary hovel built in "*lambing-time,*"
for the convenience of the shepherds in attending to
the sheep. A. S. *hulc.* Moor, For.

HULL, *n.* To throw or hurl, of which perhaps it is a
corruption. "*Hull* th' orts to the hoogs." Moor,
Hart. Ev. Wilb. Bat.

2. Whole. "Heart *hull,*" heart whole; "*hully,*"
wholly.

HULT. To open a rabbit, hare, &c. Bailey has

" to *hulk*, to take out the garbage of a hare or coney."

> " I could *hulk* your grace, and hand you up cross-leg'd,
> Like a hare at a poulter's."
>
> *B. and F. Philaster*, v. 1.

A. S. *holian*, vacuare.

HUM-CLOSEN, *s.* Home closes, *i. e.* those fields immediately adjoining the homestead or farm-house. This must by no means be confounded with the " *holms*," or " *hams*," in the valley of the Nen and other rivers. See *Norden's Delineation of Northamptonshire*, p. 37.

HUMPHREY-ROW, *s.* A violent dispute. Can this have originated in some irascible Humphrey?

HUNDRED-THISTLE. Turo eringo. Morton.

HUNDY, *s.* To injure with the horns. Bat.

HURKLE, *s.* To crouch. Clare. In Leicestershire, " To *cower* and contract the body, as in sickness." Ev. in *v.*

HUS. This word, the old A. S. form of house, is still retained when preceded by some other word denoting its use or character; thus—duf-*hus*, dove-house; hood-*hus*, a wood-house, &c. Also applied to the common sitting-room of a farm-house. Car. For. in house. Bat. *heros.*

HUST. A cough; now more frequently applied to that disorder among cattle. Ic. *hosts.* A. S. *hwosta*, tussis. Ev. Jam.

HUTCH, *n.* A coop, or large chest. Moor, Her. Ev. In old French, *huche* signified a chest or large coffer;

a word still retained in the patois of the Channel Islands. See *Cæsarea, or an Account of the Island of Jersey*, p. 44 (ed. 1835).

ING, *s.* A meadow near a brook. Ic. *einge.* Car.

INNERDS, *s.* Inwards, entrails "Pigs *innerds.*" A. S. *innewarde.* Shaks. 2 *Hen. IV.* For. Bar.

INON, *s.* An onion. Fr. *oignon.* Ak. Hart. Bar. For. Jen. *inin.*

ISTRAY, *s.* Yesterday. " I sin him *istray.*"

IT, *s.* Yet.

IT, *n.* Without the inflection for *its* : " *it* feace," " *it* mouth," &c. Ev.

JACK-A-LANTERN, *s.* " To carry *jack-a-lantern,*" *i. e.* on the shoulders.

JACK-A-LENT, *s.* A puppet formerly thrown at in Lent; now only used as a reproachful epithet, as in Shaks. *Merry Wives of Windsor*, iii. 3. *See* Oxfordshire custom, described by Kennet, in the *Camden Society's Anecdotes and Traditions*, p. 114.

JERKIN, *s.* " *Jerkin* about," romping.

JIFFY, *s.* A small space of time. " I'l dut in a *jiffy.*" Ak. Car. Tees. Bar.

JINGLES, *s.* Beads, &c., hung on, were appended to the ends of bobbins. These *jingles* are more for ornament than use, and are adopted from an ambition to make the pillow look smart. Old coins are frequently used for this purpose; hence that eyesore to antiquaries, the perforation through the rim. This

word is often used by old writers for trinkets, &c.
Vide Nares in *v*.

JINNY-BUNTAIL, *s*. The ignis fatuus, or Will with
the wisp.   Believed in Northamptonshire to proceed
from a dwarfish spirit, who takes delight in mislead-
ing "night-faring clowns," not unfrequently winding
up a long series of torments by dragging his victims
into a river or pond.   The word is evidently a corruption of *Jinn* with the *burnt tail, Jild burnt tail*.

> " Will with the wisp, or *Gyl burnt tayle*."
>> *Gayton's Notes on Don Quixote*.
>>> Lond. 1654. p. 97.

> " An ignis fatuus, or exalation, and *gillon a burnt
> tayle*, or Will with the wispe."
>> *Ibid*, p. 268.

JOIST, *n*. To graze cattle at a stipulated sum per
diem, &c.   A corruption or broad pronunciation of
the word *agist*, derived by Johnson from the Fr.
gisto, a bed or resting place.   The word is still in
every-day use, and is a Northamptonshire word of
some two centuries standing, as will be seen from the
following quotation :—

> "Borrough great fenne containeth about 7,000
> acres : this fenne is vsually so much surrounded
> that the dry places and all are not able to beare the
> inhabitants cattell ; in those two yeares (1619-1620)
> it was all dry, and yeelded such abundance of foather,
> that they received for a great part of summer 50 li
> a day for the *ioysting* of cattell, as they call it, out of
> the high countrey."
>> *Discourse concerning the Drayning of Fennes*.
>>> Lond. 1629.

JOISTER, *n.* An animal taken "to *joist.*" Ev.

JOLE, *n.* To roll to and fro in walking.

JORUM, *s.* A quantity, generally of food. For. has "*jeroboam,* or *jorum,* a capacious bowl." Jen. Hart.

KANGLE, *s.* To entangle. "That thread be *kangled.*"

KANGLIN-COMB. A wide-toothed comb. In the north a *flacking-comb.* q. v.

KANSH, *s.* A pile of faggots. "*Kansy,* a rick." Bat. In Norfolk Forby defines a *canch* to mean a small quantity of corn in the straw, put into a corner of the barn or out-house.

2. To pile wood, potatoes, &c. Ev. *kensh.*

KEAL, KALE. Pieces of stone "in very small masses, and uncertain and irregular shape." This would appear to be the genuine name for such substances. Morton says, "Whether they are pieces or shreds of the limestone, of the ragg, or of our ordinary sandstone, they have all the name of *keale.*" In some parts of the county it is more especially applied to the scalings or fragments of the sandstone, as *creach,* or *crash,* is to the limestone. Morton, p. 41. A. S. *scylan.* Sui. G. Ic. *skilia,* seperare. A. S. *scala.* Belg. *schalie,* putamina. Fr. *chaille,* a rocky earth.

KECK, *s.* To be sick. Ak. &c. Sw. *krakas.* Ic. *kvok.*

KECK-HANDED, *s.* Left-handed. Mr. Halliwell *(Dictionary of Archaic and Provincial Words)* gives this as an Oxfordshire word, and renders it "*wrongly :*" the primitive sense is, I believe, the one I have given it.

KEECH, *s.* To dip and take up water or other liquid ; to lade.

KEEP. Food for cattle. Ak. For. Bar. Hart.

KELL. The omentum of a slaughtered animal. For. Ev. Hart. A. S. *kylle*, ater.

KERCHER, *s.* A neckhandkerchief.

KERLACK, *s.* Charlock. In the northern districts *kedlock*, as in Shropshire and Leicestershire. Hart. Ev. in *v.*

KERNELS, *n.* Pyrites.

KETCH, ⎫ *s.* To congeal. " All of a *kitch*." " Those
KITCH, ⎭   coals be *kitched*." Ak.

KAINT, *s.* Cannot. " I *kaint* do it."

KID, *s.* A peascod. Bat. Bar. Sw. *kudde*. Wel. *cod.*
  2. A bundle of dry thorns, or small faggot. Marshall's East Yorkshire Glossary, Hart. Ev. Car. Wel. *cidwcln.*

KILL-DRY. The process of drying wheat, which a wet harvest has caused to " spring in the ear," or germinate. A. S. *kelan*, to cool.

KILL'S-A-FIRE, *s.* A proverbial expression, intimating the existence of enmity. " *Kill's-a-fire* 'tween they two." " The tow is in the *fire*," is another of these symbolical allusions. Both are to be found in Arthur Hall's Works. Lond. (about 1598), pp. 5 and 19.

KIMNEL, ⎫
KIMBLE, ⎭ *n.* A washing tub or tray. Hart. Ev.

KINDLY, *n.* Well to do. "A *kindly* cow." Lanc. Bat.

KINGS. An exclamation in use among boys to give notice of a cessation of game.

KINKAM, *s.* To throw a stone "*kinkam*," is to project it with just sufficient force to enable it to skim along the surface of a pond without sinking. Belg. *kink*, plica.

KIT. The entire quantity, "the whole *kit*." For. Moor, Car. Jam. Hart. I have also heard the term applied to denote collectively a number of families of the same name; among which, although, individually speaking, all traces of relationship may have become extinct, a kind of ideal clanship still exists, never more observable than in the broils and pugnacious manifestations which are continually occurring to disturb the harmony of the feast-day. Clearly and legitimately derived from the A. S. *kythe.*

KIT-CAT, *n.* A pellucid vitrified stone, used to stanch blood, hence often called staunch or staund stone. At Kettering it has given name to a lane, so called from its having been found there in great abundance. Bridges in *Kettering.*

KITLIN. A kitten. Common to the Anglian dialects.

KIT-WILLOW. The almond-leaved willow. Morton.

KIVVER. To cover. Wilb. For. Hart. *kever.*

    2 A round wooden tub or tray used in making butter. Fr. *cuvier.*

KLEEF, *s.* Generally the appellation of a field on the steep side of a hill. A. S. *clif,* clivus. Old Germ. *klief,* oblique.

KNACKER, *n.* A village harness mender. For.

KNAVE, *n.* A familiar name for the black-bird : the children's gloss on its cry being—

"Draw the *knave* a cup of beer ;
Be quick, quick, quick !"

Clare.

KNOP, *n.* A bud or blossom. Dan. *knop.* Germ. *knoepe.* Teut. *knoppe.* Jam.

KNOTS, *n.* The name of a variety of pyrites. Morton, p. 117.

KOTTLED. Perplexed. Bat. *kotlerd.*

LACE-SONGS. A name given to a curious variety of rhymes, sung at the lace-pillow. The burdens, stanza, &c., so arranged as to assist the young worker in completing the various movements of the bobbins. Lace making is almost always accompanied with singing, and on passing through a village on a summer's day, the sight of the knitters and lacemakers grouped on the green, working and chanting " in the sun," cannot fail to recal to the memory those lines of our great poet—

" ———— it is old and plain :
The spinsters, and the knitters in the sun,
And the free maids, that weave their thread with
    bones,
Do use to chant it : it is silly, sooth,
And dallies with the innocence of love,
Like the old age."

Twelfth Night, ii. 4.

LADE, *n.* Synonymous with *keech.* A. S. *hladan.* Tees. Bar. *liade.*

LADE-SKIP. A brewing utensil used in "*lading,*" or

transferring the beer from one tub to another. A. S. *hladan*, haurire; *sciop*, vas.

LADY-LOCK, *s*. The ladybird.

LAMB. To beat or otherwise ill-treat. Wilb. Car. Hart. Ic. *lam*, cædo. *Arthur Hall's Works*, p. 98 (rep. 1814).

LAMB-EARTH. A variety of dark-coloured vegetable soil. A corruption probably of *loam*. Germ. *lehm*.

LAMB-TOE. The kidney vetch.

LAND-SPRING. A spring of the temporary kind. Morton, p. 318.

LARENCE. An imaginary being, supposed to preside over idle people. Invoked sometimes as "*Long Larence*," a phrase common to most parts of the kingdom. I am not aware that St. Lawrence has ever claimed the patronship of this class of persons, though we are told by Naogeorgus (B. Googe's translation), p. 98, that—

> "*Laurence*, from the backe, and from the shoulders, sicknesse puttes."

LARGESS, *n*. A gift to reapers in harvest.

LASH, LUSH, { *n*. Juicy, rank : applied to a meadow causing cattle to be *lash* or loose. For. "*Lashe*, laxus. Prompt. Parv. Mins. *lashe*."

> "How *lush* and lusty the grass looks."
>
> *Tempest*, ii. 1.

LASH-HORSE, *s*. The second horse in a team.

LATER, LOITER. { The number of eggs laid by the hen before she begins to sit. Broc. *lawter*. Jam. *lachter*. For. *latter*. Jen. *laiter*. Teut. *leghtyd*, tempus quo gallinæ puriant.

LATH, *s.* Loth. A. S. *lat.*

LAUND, *n.* A land; the space between two furrows.
2. A lawn. Chaucer. Dan. *land.* Shaks. *Venus and Adonis.*

LAYER, *n.* Pasturage for sheep, &c.; applied to the land on which they lie. Teut. *lægher.* Germ. *læger.*

> " Have the winters been so set
> To raine and snowe, they have wet
> All his driest *laire ;*
> By which means his sheep have got
> Such a deadly carelesse rot,
> That none living were."
> *Browne's Shepherd's Pipe.* Lond. 1614.

LAYERD, *s.* Laid, as corn beaten down by rain or wind. Hart. *loaged.* A. S. *logian,* componere.

LAY-LANDS, *n.* Arable land which has been suffered to " *lay down*" to grass. Car. Tees.

LAY'T, *s.* An idiomatic expression, to " *lay out,*" or predict. " I *lay't* it 'l be a fine day."

LEAF, *n.* The fat adjoining the kidney of a pig. Hart. Ev.

LEAM, *n.* A drain or watercourse in the fenny districts.

LEAN, *n.* Sterile, applied to land.

LEARS, *s.* Long sticks used in making hedges.

LEASE, *s.* To glean. The use of this word is one of the principal distinguishing features of the western dialects. In South Northamptonshire, Oxfordshire, and Buckinghamshire, it is in common use, but totally disappears as we proceed in a northern or eastern direction. A. S. *lesan.*

LEASE. A pasture field. A. S. *læs.* Tees.

LEAVE-GO. Let loose. "He wouldn't *leave-go.*"

LEECH. The apparatus for running lye; hence "to set the *leech.*" Moor. Germ. Teut. *lauge.* Bel. *looghs,* lye.

LEECH-TUB. A vessel to catch the lye as it percolates through the *leech.* In the Staffordshire salt-works, a *leech*-trough is the vessel through which the salt is allowed to drain, the produce thus obtained being called *leech*-brine.—*Plot's Natural History of Staffordshire,* p. 92. For. *lie-latch.* Jen. *lie-lip.*

LIEFER, *n.* Rather. "*Liefer* you nor me." Car. Tees. Hart. *liever.*

LIFT, *n.* A course or layer of limestone strata. Morton.

LIG, *n.* A lie. "*Ligster,* a liar." Bat. Ev. Belg. *lieghen.*

LIKE. "A word," says Batchelor, "often added to a phrase without improving or adding to the meaning of it," as, "I didn't know what a wur to do, I was so mammerd *like.*" Doubtless intended by the users as an expletive, but having quite the contrary effect to a person unacquainted with the peculiarity. Evidently the A. S. *lice,* often used in that language for converting the verb or substantive into the adjective. Hart. For. Bat.

LIKELY. Thriving, prosperous; as a "*likely* yow." Car. Tees. Jam. Dan. *lykkelig.*

LIKE-SHENCE, *s.* Likelihood. "No *like-shence* of his coming to-day."

LINKS, *n.* A tract of heath, or "*ling*" land. Dan. *lyng.* Ic. *ling*, erica.

LESSOM. Nimble, "*lithesome.*" Ak. Jen. Bar.

LIVE-EARTH, *n.* Common vegetable mould. " Our husbandmen call it the heart of the land, and the *live-earth*, as it is the substance and life of vegetables." Morton, p. 30.

LIVE-LODE. Income, livelihood. A good old word. Nares.

> "As well of wordly *live-lode* as of life."
> *Spencer's Moth. Hub. Tale*, v. 145.
> "John a Stile hath 2000 acres in the fen, worth him, haply, 50 li a yeere, and no other *live-lode.*"
> *Discourse concerning the Drayning of Fennes,*
> Lond. 1629.

LIVING, *n.* A farm or tenement. The common fields in most parishes were divided into "*livings.*"

LOCK, *s.* "A *lock* of hay," "A *lock* of wool," &c.; used in the same manner as if speaking of hair. Ak. Jen. Her. Barret.

LODGE, *s.* A very frequent designation of a lone farm-house.

LOLLUP, *s.* To lounge, or *loll* idly about. Bat. Car.

LONG-PURPLES. The purple loose-strife.

> "There with fantastic garlands did she make,
> Of crow-flowers, nettles, daisies, and *long-purples.*"
> *Hamlet*, iv. 6.

LOOM, *n.* The well in which the hogs' wash is kept. A. S. *loma*, utensilia. Jam. *loom*, a tub.

LOVE-KNOTS, *n.* A divination performed [with blades of grass. Vide *Clare's Shep. Cal.* p. 184.

LOWBELL, *s.* When a peasant of South Northamptonshire has committed any glaring breach of good morals, it is customary for his neighbours to "*lowbell*" him ; the meaning of which is best expressed by its apparent etymology, the past participle of the A. S. *Lowian,* and the verb *bellan* (still retained in this dialect, *vide* BELL). On the first appearance of the culprit in "*strit,*" or on "*grin,*" the villagers rise *en masse,* and greet him with a terrible din of tin pots and kettles, &c. ; and amidst the hooting and vociferation of the multitude he is generally compelled to seek shelter by flight. This is called "*lowbelling,*" and the actors are termed "*lowbells,*" or "*lowbellers,*" forming a tolerable explanation of the "*lowbell*" in *Beaumont and Fletcher's Woman's Prize,* act i. sc. 3. which has so long mystified the commentators :—

> "PETRU. If you can carry't so, 'tis very well.
> BIAN. No, you shall carry it, sir.
> PETRU. Peace, gentle *Lowbell.*"

Biancha, "the commander-in chiefe," has before irritated Petruchio with her sarcastic allusions and taunts, and her interference in the present instance produces the impatient, "Peace, gentle "*lowbell.*"

LUMBER, *s.* To thump, drop, or beat with a heavy sound. "To *lumber* the door." "Kick up a *lumber,*" *i. e.* make a great disturbance.

LUMMAKIN, *s.* Awkward. "A great *lummakin* fellow."

LUMP, *s.* A few, or small quantity ; not confined, as the dictionaries have it, to a "shapeless mass."

F

LUMPING, *n.* The stroke of the flail in threshing.

> "The thresher, once *lumping*, we heard him no more."
>
> *Clare's Village Minstrel,* p. 31.

Teut. *lomper*, infligere.

MACE, *s.* A friend or companion. A. S. *maca.* In the northern dialects, *make.*

MADE, *n.* Stolen. An old cant word. C. "I *made* this knife at a heat," *i. e.* stole it cleverly. Ev.

MAGGING, *s.* Disputing. "They two be allas *maggin.*" For. has it in the sense of to chatter. Bat. *mag*, to tease.

MAKINS. A common asseveration. Probably a diminution of "*By the mass.*" Randolph puts this oath into the mouth of Agroicus.—*Muses' Looking Glass*, iv. 4.

> "I would not have my zonne Dick one those Boets for the best pig in my stye, by the *mackins.*"

In *Cole's* "*Preservatives against Sinne,*" Lond. 1618, among "ridiculous oaths derived from greater, which the parties are ashamed to utter," he places "by the *maskins,* for "*by the mass.* By *cock,* for by *God,* &c." An amusing collection of oaths may be found in *Powell's* "*Summons for Swearers,*" Lond. 1645, where, among other "store of cannon shot for battering to pieces this mouth-defiling, ear-infecting, soul-killing, land-shaking sin," he strongly reprehends the custom men have of "mincing their oaths, as if God would not espy them when as man may, as ' By Dickens, *maskins,* s'lid, barlady's foot,' &c." "Come into the country," says he, p. 38, "and you shall see the silliest one wise enough to this evil, and that the rudest in speech can be eloquent in blasphemy."

MALTER, MOULTER.

To melt, dissolve, or become pulverized ; also a word addressed to a person to bid him depart quickly. Ex. " Now, you sir, *malter!* " *i. e.* vanish. *melt*, begone! A person describing the appearance of a ghost, said, " It stopped a minute and then *malter'd.*" A. S. *meltan*, liquefacere. For. has *molted*, violently affected by heat ; *molt*, clear exsudation. Moor has " *multa*, land laid in ridges exposed to the air and frost, that it may become pulverized and fine, when next ploughed, is said to *multa*, or be laid to *multa*. Jen. the verb *malt*, to melt.

" MOLTER. Verm. D. Rubi Chamæmori quos alias Hjortron appellamus ab Vermelandis, vero rectius non nisi Rubi adeo maturi, ut fere sint liquidi, *Molter*, nominantur, quo eosdem Jemptlandi Mytha Myrbar vocum. A. Saxon *molten*, liquefactus."

Dissertatio Philogia de Dialectis Svio. Goth. 1761.

In the North German dialects they call *multer* anything reduced to powder, dust, &c. *Noehden's Dict.* in *v.*

MAMMERD, *s.* Perplexed, confused. " I was so *mammerd.*" In North N. *moitherd.* Car.

MANNIKEN. A small child, or dwarfish person. A

diminutive of man, or from the Wel. *man*. Fr. *mignon*, parva. Shaks. C.

MANG, *n*. A confused mixture. " All in a *mang*." A. S. *mengan*. Sui. G. *menga*, miscere. Ev. In Teesdale the same name is given to a mash of bran.

MARCHAND, MARCHANT. { A merchant : applied in a more extended sense than in city phraseology. Fr. *marchand*.

" A *marchant* was ther with a forked berd."
Chau. Prologue to Cant. Tales, 254.

MARKET-STEAD, *n*. A market-place. A. S. *stead*, a place.

MASLIN, *n*. A mixture of wheat and rye. Car. Tees.

MATTY, *n*. Matted, interwoven.

MAUNDER. To grumble or threaten. Com. " *Maunders*, beggars." C.

MAUNT, *s*. Must not.

MAUNTLY, *s*. Greatly, very much. " I should *mauntly* like to see it."

MAVIS, *n*. The singing thrush. Bat. For. Jam. Fr. *mauvis*.

MAWKIN, *n*. A scarecrow. Hart. Ev. C. Jen. Also a kind of mop used in cleaning an oven. Ak. For. Bar. Minsheu has " *malkin, maukin*, to make clean an oven.

MAWMSY. A trifling, foolish fellow. Jam. *mawsie*, scortum. Ic. *masa*, vagor. Ev.

MAYS-GOLD. A child's game, much like the *Merry ma-tanzie* described by *Chambers' Popular Rhymes of Scotland*, p. 268 (ed. 1847).

MAZE, *s.* To bewilder. "A clane *mazed* me," he quite astonished me. A. S. *masa*, a whirpool.

MAZZARD, *s.* The head. Ak. Her. Shaks. *Othello*, ii. 3; *Hamlet*, v. 1. Hence a "*mazzard*-oak," a headed one.

MEASTER,
MAESTER, } *s.* Master. The pronunciation is most in conformity with the A. S. In the northern district *maister* is the word used.

MEBBY, *s.* It may be. "*Mebby* 'twunt, *mebby* 'twull," perhaps it will not, perhaps it will. Similar to the French *peut-être*, the it being in both cases understood. Jen. Car. Tees.

MEDLANDS, *n.* Meadow lands.

MESS. A number or quantity. Bat.

2. The number of rabbits found in a burrow.

MIFF, *s.* Offence. "To take *miff*." Bar. Jen.

MILE. Miles. Nouns of weight and measure pass unchanged into the plural. Car. Her. For.

> "From south to north he ys long eigte hundred
> *myle*."
>
> *Robert of Gloucester*, p. 1.

MILLARD, *s.* A miller. Ak.

2. A name given to a large species of white moth. Bar. For. *millar*.

MIMMOCKIN, *n.* An epithet applied to a small weakly child or animal. Her. For. in *minnock*.

MOARZE, *n.* To burn without flame.

MOLLIN, *s.* A leathern bridle for carthorses. Ic. *mull*. Sui. G. *myl*.

MOON, *s* To stare.

MOOR, *n.* A kind of peat, being a vegetable substance in a partial state of decay, formed by a congeries of the roots and fibres of many species of plants mixed with earthy matter.

MOORY-LAND, *n.* A black, light, and loose earth, without any stones, and with very little clay or sand intermixed. Morton, p. 36.

MOP. A fair at which servants are hired. Her. Ak.

MOOT-HILL, *n.* Many hills in the valley of the Welland, and other parts of the county, are thus designated. They are supposed to be the ancient *Folk-mote hills*, to which the country people were wont to resort for consultation, &c., when any danger threatened their district. The town-house in some of our towns is called the *moot-hall. Morton*, p. 546.

MORRIS DANCE. The Morris dance is performed in Northamptonshire by six or eight young men, gaily decked out with ribands, buttons, &c., and with a great number of little bells attached to their legs; each carries in his hands a strong round stick, of about a yard in length. The dance, which is of the most picturesque character, consists of a series of rapid evolutions, changes of posture, &c., accompanied with brandishing and clashing of the staves and flourishing of kerchiefs. The clown, or " Tom Fool," has generally an old quilt thrown over him, plentifully hung with rabbit-skins; his cap is ornamented with a feather, and in his hand he holds a stick with an inflated bladder attached to the end by a cord.

This, together with the piper, completes the set. A more picturesque and thoroughly English scene can scarcely be imagined than a performance of this kind under the trees of a village green. This description of the fool tallies well with the account given by Strutt from the *Illuminators* of the 13th century.—*View of the Dress and Manners of Engand*, vol. ii. p. 313.

MORT, *n.* A quantity. Thus Clare—

> "Then shouts of rods, and *morts* of threats besides,
> Picture harsh truths in his unpractised breast."
>
> *Shep. Cal.* p. 69.

Johnson gives the Ic. *marght*, multum. A. S. *mærth*, vis. Bat. Ev.

MOT, *s.* A moat, or small pond. Fr. *motte*.

MOTHERY, *s.* Mouldy, or thick, as stale beer. Dut. *moeder*. Ak. Bar.

MOULT, *n.* A moth. Ev. Bat. Dut. *motte*.

> "Nile ye tresoure to you tresouris in erthe : where rust and *moughts* distrieth, and where theues deluen out and stelen."
>
> *Wicliffe, Matthew*, c. vi. v. 19.

MOW, or MOWFEN, { *n.* A name formerly given to a fen which in the summer-time yielded fodder for cattle.

MOIL. To toil, labour hard. To be found in Johnson and the other dictionaries, but obsolete in composition. Ev. Car. For.

> "I *moyle* and toyle for ye ; I am your hackney."
>
> *B. and F. Women Pleased*, ii. 4.

In the Exmoor dialect, a "*moil*" is a mule, and to "*moily*," is to toil like those patient animals.

MUDDER. Mother. Germ. *mutter*. Sw. *moder*.

MUGGY. Mouldy. Dan. *muggen*. Sw. *moglig*.

MUGGY-WEATHER, *s.* Dull, misty weather. Wel. *mwg*, smoke, fume, &c.

MULLOCK. Rubbish. Chaucer, Com.

MULTER, *n.* To moulder. Sw. *multna*. Sui. G. *mull*, pulvis. For. *mulder*. Moor, *multa*.

MULLS, *n.* This word, when quickly repeated, is used to call the cows to be milked.

MULLY, *n.* To bellow as a cow. "How that keow *mullys*." Ic. *mogla*. Germ. *muhen*, mugire.

MULLY-COW. Used by children, and also when cows are spoken of to children. Correlatives may be found in Tees. in *v.* coddy, giss, &c.

MUMMERS. Masqueraders, who go from house to house on St. Andrew's night (O. S.), and continued during Christmas. *Vide* Tander.

MUN, *n.* Must; also pronounced *maun*. "Ye *mun* do it." Wicliffe has *mowne*. Ic. *mun*. Jam. Hart. Car.

    2. A common expletive; perhaps a corruption of man, but used in speaking to a female, or even a dog. Ak. Bat. Ex. It is amusing to note how seldom, among the uneducated classes, occur the phrases "husband and wife." A woman always speaks of her husband as "her *man*," and a man often designates his wife as "his *oman*."

MUXY, *s.* Dirty. Sui. G. *mock*, firmus.

NAISH, } *s.* Tender, delicate, dainty.   Ev.   Wilb.
NASH, }   *nesh.*   Germ: *naschen,* to be dainty.

NAN, *s.* What did you say? signifying that the speaker has not heard or understood what is said to him; now almost obsolete, or used only by "the oldest inhabitants." Boucher considers this to be a reduplication of the A. S. particle *an,* which is defined to be " particula interrogationibus præmissa." Brocket conjectures the Fr. interrogation *ain,* and For. derives it from the A. S. *nean,* prope.

NAP, *n.* To catch or lay hold of.   Sw. *nappa.*

NAPPY, *n.* Ale. From the adjective "*nappy,*" which Palsgrave renders "vigoreux."

> " A bonne, God wote !
> Stickes in my throate
> Without I have a draught
> Of cornie aile,
> *Nappy* and staile."
> *Wright's Christmas Carols,* p. 107.

NARRA, *s.* Neither.   "*Narra* you nor I."

NAR. 2. Never. " Ye'll *narra* a'rt," You'll never have it.   A. S. *næfre.*   Germ. *nie.*

NAR, *n.* Near.   Dan. *nœhr.*   Wilb.

NARRA-ONE, } *s.* Never a one, neither of them.
NARRUN, }

NARSIN. Never since. " I bent sin un *narsin* istray," I have not seen him since yesterday.

NAUNTLE, *n.* To elevate.

NAVE. *s.* An arrangement of sticks attached to a rick, in order to form a resting place for the bundles of straw while thatching. Mr. Halliwell gives this as an Oxfordshire word.

NEAR. Mean, parsimonious. Dan. *gnier*. For. Her. Bar.

NEITHER HERE NOR THERE. Nothing to the purpose. Ev.

NEST, *n.* Next. "*Nest* to that." A. S. *nehst*. Hart. Car.

NETTLE-MONGER. The reed-sparrow; so called from its frequenting nettles.

NEXT-WAYS, ⎱ *n.* Directly. "I'll go *next-ways.*"
NEST-WIZZ, ⎰ Ev. Bat.

NIFFLE, *s.* To swallow hastily. "*Niffle* it down."

NIGH-HAND, *s.* Probably, most likely. "He'll come *nigh-hand* to-night." "Where be you goin to-day?" "To Oundle, *nigh-hand.*" Ev. Bat.

NINE-PEG-MORRIS. A game similar to the *Nine men's morris* mentioned by Shaks. *Mid. Night's Dream*, ii. 2; upon which Farmer remarks in a note: "In that part of Warwickshire where Shakspeare was educated, and the neighbouring parts of Northamptonshire, the shepherds and other boys dig up the turf with their knives to represent a sort of imperfect chess-board. It consists of a square, sometimes only a foot diameter, sometimes three or four yards. Within this is another square, every side of which is parallel to the external square; and these squares are joined by lines drawn from each corner of both squares, and the middle of each line. One party or player has wooden pegs, the other stones, which they move in such a manner as to take up each other's "*men*," as they are called. These figures are by the country people called *Nine men's morris*, or *merrils*, and are so called because each party has nine men." For the probable etymology see *Brand's Popular Antiquities*, ii. p. 253 ; *Douce's Illustrations of Shakespeare*, p. 114 (ed. 1839).

NITLE. Clever, sharp. "A *nitle* chap." Ev. Perhaps the Teut. *nett*, our *neat*.

NOAH'S-ARK. A form of the clouds supposed to resemble that object.

NO-HOW, *s*. Any way. " I kaint dut *no-how*."

NO-SENSE. Not good. "*No-sense* of a job." " I don't feel *no-sense* to-day," *i. e.* not very well.

NUBBIN, *n*. The stump of a tree after the trunk has been felled. Ev.

NUDGELIN. Tough and hardy. " A *nudgelin* chump of a boy."

NUNCHIN, *s*. The noon meal. *Noon* in this dialect is always sounded *nun*. A. S. *nun*. Ak. Bar. *nunch*. For. *noonings*.

ODD-HOUSE, *n*. A solitary house. A Leicestershire provincialism. Ev. in *v*. In the south "*luon-house*."

ODDMENTS, *n*. Additions, odds. Jam. Tees. Car. For. Jen.

OFF, *n*. From. " I bought it *off* him." Ev.

OFF-HIS-HEAD, *n*. A phrase applied to a deranged person. Ev.

OLD. Wold is thus pronounced. The village of Wold

is invariably so called, and so the old local riddle rhyme—

"The wind blows cold upon Yardly *old*."

This spelling is followed by Shaks. *Lear*, iii. sc. 4.

OR,
WHOR, An imperative, commanding the fore-horse of a team to bear towards the driver. Car. in *hauve*. Hart. *haw*. For other terms of the Houyhmnn dialect see *heit*, *woot*, &c.

ORTINS, *n.* Leavings. Formed from *ort*, a good old word, used provincially in most parts of England.

OSIER-HOLT, *n.* An osier-bed. Ev.

OST. To offer or attempt. Car. *osse*. Ev. Wilb. Hunt. *ause*.

OUTINGS. Rejoicings, feasting, &c.

OUT-WRIGHT. A bagman, or travelling dealer; also the journeymen of a master carpenter who go out to the various farms for employment. A. S. *ut*, out; *woryhta*, operarius.

OVER-GET. To get over. "He must *over-get* his disappointment." Ev.

OVER-GO. To remove, or get away from. "To *over-go* a village," is to pass through it. Ev. has the word among his Leicestershire provincialisms in a somewhat similar sense. A. S. *ofer-gan*, to pass beyond, &c.

OVER-LONG, *s.* Long since. "*Over-long* ago." Dut. *over-lange*.

OVER-MINDED, *s.* Much inclined. "He warn't *overminded* to du't."

OVERTHWART, *n.* Lapped over, or across. Sw.
ofwer-twert.

OVER-WARTS. Across, opposite. Ev. A corruption, probably, of *over-wards.* Ev.

OVVER, *n.* Often pronounced *uvver.* Upper. "The
ovver one of the two." Germ. &c. *ober.* Villages
whose situation would in S. Hants have procured
them the prefix of "*upper,*" are in the northern and
midland districts termed *over.* The Frisian island
of Heligoland is divided into Unter and *Ober*-land.

OXBALL. A round hairy ball frequently found in the
stomach of an ox.

PACKWACK. The gristly tendons of the neck of
animals.

PAD, *n.* A path. Dut. *pad.* Also applied to the
impress of the feet upon soft ground; hence to make
a path. A. S. *pethian.*

PADD, *s.* To work with the paddle.

PADDLE, *s.* A species of spud, used for the purpose
of eradicating weeds.—*Deuteronomy,* chap. xxiii.
13.

PALM, *n.* The English palm or sallow. In all probability so called from the circumstance of its having
been used to decorate churches on Palm Sunday, as
a substitute for branches of the real tree. Bridges,
speaking of Cliffe Regis, informs us that on Palm
Sunday the church is adorned with palm-branches
in the seats and windows. Marshall, in his *Rural
Economy of Yorkshire* (Lond. 1788), describes palms
as the "male catkins of the sallow, which are worn

in the hat (if the season permit) on Palm Sunday."
Car. Wilb. Tees.

PANCAKE-BELL. "On Shrove Tuesday, at noon,
it is the custom to ring one of the bells of the church,
which is called the '*pancake-bell*,' a joyful sound to
all the youngsters of the village, intimating a holiday
and sport."—*Cole's History of Weston Favell.* Scarb.
1827, p. 57.

PANCHEON, *n.* A large earthenware pan, wide at
the top and gradually narrowing. Ev.

PARGE, *n.* To plaster. Fr. *pargeter.*

> " From *pargetting*, painting, slicking, glazing, and
> renewing old rivelled faces,
>> Good Mercury defend us." ·
>>> *Jonson's Cynthia's Revels.*

PAULT, *s.* Weeds, squitch, &c. A contraction of
"*pulled out*," *i. e.* that which is "*pult*," or pulled
out.

PATTIKEYS, *n.* The seed-vessels of the ash. Tees.
catskeys. Germ. *katze.*

PEAKIN, *n.* Sickly looking. Moor, Ev. "He
looked but *peakin.*"

PED, *n.* A pannier. For.

PEDGEL, *n.* To chaffer or deal, as a pedlar; or
"*.pedgely.*" Ev.

PEEK, *s.* To peep. An old word found in Palgrave.
" I seed un *peekin* throw the kay-hul."

PEEP, *n.* A young sprout or shoot just peeping from
the earth. "A cowslip *peep*," &c. According to
our lexicographers this word has some affinity with
the Fr. *pepier*, the sound which chickens make upon

the first breaking of the shell (Cotgrave in *v.*) being
applied to the action. The verb *peep* is often used
by our writers to express the first visible appearance
of germination.

> "So the broad oak, which from thy grand design
> Shall spread aloft, and tell the world 'twas thine,
> A stripling first, just *peep'd* above the ground,
> Which, ages hence, shall fling its shade around."
>
> *Lloyd to Rev. Mr. Hanbury.*

> " And as they *peep* forth of the ground and ripen
> first, so they first dye away and disappear."
>
> *Morton*, p. 53.

PELT. The undressed skin of a sheep. Lat. *pellis.*
Germ. *peltz*, a skin. For. Her.

2. A rage, or short ebullition of temper. Ak. Bar. C.

PENDLE, *n.* A hard lumpish kind of stone. Morton.

PENNY. " To live by the *penny.*" To be constantly
in the habit of purchasing the necessaries of life, as
opposed to the old custom of consuming one's own
produce.

> " In Northamptonshire all the rivers of the
> county are bred in it; besides those (Ouse and Char-
> well) it lendeth and sendeth into other shores : so
> the good housekeeper hath a fortune of wheat in his
> fields, mutton in his fold, &c., both to serve himself
> and supply others. The expense of a feast will but
> breath him, which will tire another of the same
> estate who buys all by the *penny.*"
>
> *Fuller's Holy and Profane State*, 1642, pp. 153-4.

PENNY-GRASS. The common yellow coxcomb; the
seed-vessels of the plant are round and flat, resembling pence, which accounts for the designation. In

Sweden, from the same reason, it is called *penning-gras*.

PENNY-SHELLS. A name given to a species of Nummulite, found abundantly in some parts of the county. The soil in which they are most found is called *penny-earth*.

PEN-PARLOR, *s.* A secure place, a place where any one is *penned* in; also used figuratively to express a difficult or perplexing position. "I be in such a "*pen-parlor*."

PEN-THRUSH, *s.* The largest species of thrush (*Turdus viscivorus*), called in the northern districts the *mist*, or *mizzle-thrush*. In the ancient British and modern Welsh languages, *Pen* signifies *head*, or *chief*. The Welsh call this bird "*pen y llwyn*," the head, or master of the coppice, an epithet which he is fully entitled to from his pugnacious propensities. Here we have a still surviving relic of the "*Wealh cynne*."

PETH, *s.* Pith.

PETTICHAP, *n.* The long-tailed titmouse.

PICK, *s.* A point, the prong of a fork, &c. A. S. *piic*, a small pin or needle.

     2. The corner of a field. Triangular fields are thus denominated in true Saxon phrase. "Three-pick closen."

PIECE. A field or tract of land, as town-*piece*, David's-*piece*, &c.

PIGGLE. To root up potatoes by the hand. This is given as a Northamptonshire word by Mr. Halliwell, on whose authority it is admitted here.

PIKE, *n.* To pick. "To *pike* the dirt off a spade." M. Ev. *poik,* as it is sometimes pronounced in this county.

PIKED, } Pointed. "A *picked* stick."
PICKED. }

PIKE-HOLE. An aperture in the wall of a barn for giving light.

PIKES, *n.* Haycocks. Car. Tees.

PILL. To peel. Dan. *pille.* Ev.

> "This I will say, that man is borne naked into the world, Homo nudus in nuda homo, hath not so much as senseless creatures, a *pille,* rinde, or barke, to defend him from the insulting violence of the sunne."
>
> *Purchas's Microcosmos.* Lond. 1619.

PINDER, *n.* A person whose duty it is to impound all stray cattle. For. Clare. A. S. *pyndan,* to inclose.

PINK, *n.* The chaffinch. Struck off on the onomatopoetic principle.

PINT, *n.* To drink a pint. Clare.

PISSEMMOTS, *s.* Ants. Belg. *pis-emme.* Hart. *pissannat.*

PIT-HOLE. A pit. Ev.

PIX, } A pick-axe.
PICK. }

PLACK. A small plot of ground, sometimes limited, as in Leicestershire, to about five yards square. Ev.

PLACKET, *n.* A pocket. For. Moor. See a disquisition on this word in *Mr. Halliwell's Dictionary of Archaic and Provincial Words.*

G

PLASH, PLEACH. { To trim or lop trees, hedges, &c.; also applied to the forming a hedge by partially cutting the upright shoots near the ground, and intertwining them between upright stakes.

"Cut vines and osier ;
  Plash hedge of enclosure."
  Tusser Feby's Husbandrie.

Moor. Her. Ev.

PLASH, *n.* A puddle; or in a more extended sense, a pool. Teut. *plasch,* palus. Hart. Ev.

PLAT, *n.* The broad level side of a stratum of stone. Dan. *plat,* planus. Germ. *platte,* a flag-stone.

PLAZEN, *s.* Plural of place. "I dwun't like they *plazen.*"

PODDOCK, PUDDOCK, { *n.* A frog. A. S. *pad.* Dan. *padde,* bufo, though never applied to that animal in England. Jam.

PODDOCK-MOON, *n.* " In, or very near, the month of August, in the hottest part of the year, for about four weeks together, frogs very rarely or never open their mouths, are never heard to croak, and their bodies appear very much swell'd; upon which account the time wherein this usually happens has, with our country people, the name of *poddock-moon.* 'Tis a thing observ'd by almost every body here, and the matter of fact is indisputable; but 'tis generally looked upon as very strange and unaccountable."— *Morton,* p. 441.

POKE, *n.* A bag. "A puddin *poke.*" A. S. *pocca.* Ic. *poki.* Car. Wilb. Tees. For. C.

POOTHY-WEATHER, *n.* A close and hot state of the atmosphere.

POOTY, *n.* A snail-shell. Clare.

POST. A layer of stone. Morton. Called also *stocks* and *benches.*

POT-BELLY, *s.* A disease among animals, consisting of an expansion of the intestines. Wel. *potena,* to swell out the belly.

POTHER. To puff, as a person after violent exercise. " A jist did *pother* some." Wel. *poth,* that which is puffed or blown out.

POUCHY. Sulky, sullen. From *pout.*

POWER. A great number. " A *power* of folk." Ev. For.

PROG. A short pointed stick.

    2. To poke or grope with such; hence "*progglin,*" meddling, prying. There is the Dan. *brod,* a goad. Moor, For. Ev.

PUDDING. A compound of barley-flour and milk, given to poultry.

PUDDLE, *s.* To labour assiduously without making much progress.

PUDDOCK, *n.* The kite or fork-winged buzzard. A. S. *pud.*

PUDGE, *n.* A puddle.

PUDROOM, *s.* A fungus, or toadstool. A. S. *pad,* a toad; *swam,* a tuber or fungus. Dut. *paddestoel,* fungus.

PUG. A sheep of half a year's growth. Bat.

PUNDER. A crossbar that hinders the body of the cart from falling backwards when loaded. Sui. G.

pundare, statera. For. has *punder*, to be exactly on an equipoise.

PUNISH. To pain. Ev. A. S. *pinan*. "A sim'd ankammon del *punish'd* wi 's bad feet."

PUNN. To bruise or pound. A. S. *punian*, conterere.

PURE, *s.* Very, extremely. "A *pure* hot day." "A *pure* hard tater."

PUTE, } The lapwing, so called from its peculiar
PEWIT. } cry. Ak. Bar. *pewit.*

QUEACHY. Same as CREACHY. *q. v.*

QUICK-ROCK. A mass of stone in strata; in other words, the "*living rock*," there being a notion, yet far from becoming extinct, that all stones owe their formation from progressive growth. A. S. *cwiccan*, to make alive. *Quick* is used by Chaucer in a like sense.

> "Not fully *quik*, ne fully dede they were."
> *Knightes Tale*, v. 1017

Morton, p. 113.

QUOCKEND. Choked. "A'most *quockend.*" Bat. Ev.

QUOT, *n.* A small boil or pustule. Ev.

QUIRK, *n.* To turn quickly.

QUITCH. *See* SQUITCH. This is nearest the A. S. *cwice.*

RAFFLE, *n.* Refuse. A. S. *reaf*, spoila. Ev. For. *rafe.*

RAFFLING. Wild, unsteady, rambling. "A *rafflin* fellow." Ic. *raf-a*, vagari. For. Ev.

RAMMER, } *n.* To exaggerate. "He does *ram*
RAM, } that out finely." Teut. *ræmen*, ex-
tendere.

RAKE, *n.* To move about, as a person in a restless
state. A woman described her invalid friend as
"very narvus, awlus *rakin* up and down the room."
Ev. Ic. *reka*, propellere, quatere. Sui. G. *reka*,
vagari.

RAME, *n.* To rave or shout violently. "Don't go to
rame out like that" A. S. *hreaman*. Sui. G.
rauma. Ic. *ryma*, clamare. Jam. Lanc. *ream.*

RAMLIN. Clumsy, &c. "He did the job after a
ramlin fashion." Sui. G. *ramla*, tumultuari. Teut.
rammel-en, strepere.

RAM-STRAM, *s.* Disorderly. Teut. *rammen*, salire.

RAMMEL, *n.* A kind of real. Morton.

RARE, *n.* To *rear* up, as the earth before the plough.

RARE, } Underdone. "*Reer* meat." A. S. *hrere.*
REERE. } Ak. Bar. Tees.

RANCH. To scratch deeply and severely. A Northamptonshire rustic would have had no difficulty in
understanding that line of "*Glorious John*" which so
puzzled the learned Johnson :—

"*Ranched* his hips with one continued wound."

Dryden, be it remembered, was a Northamptonshire
man, and he might have heard the word during one
of his many sojourns in that county.

RATTENHOOD, *i. e.* rotten wood, touchwood.

RATTS, *n.* Rags, tatters, &c. "All to *ratts.*" Teut.
rete, incisura.

RAW. Cold and watery; spoken of clayey soils.

READ, *n.* The rennet or ventricle of a cow. Bar. Bat.

REAVING, *s.* } The frame-work round a waggon.
RATHING, *n.* }   1 Bat.   2. Ev.

RED-CAP, { *s.* A wood sprite, the remembrance of whom is still kept up in the popular
RED-MAN, { legends of the peasantry. *Vide* FOLK-LORE.

REDDER, *n.* A person who endeavours to settle a dispute, adjust differences, &c. Ev. Jam. A. S. *rœtan*, liberare.

REDDIPOLE, *s.* The smoke pole of a chimney, to which the " *racks,*" or irons, are attached.

RED-EYE. A species of red sallow, concerning which there is a superstition that a branch hung up over the hearth preserves the cattle from disease, &c.   I have only met with this superstition in one instance; it may, therefore, be of foreign importation.

RED-LAND " is a term much used by our husband-men here, and in neighbouring counties; and though the name is expressive of no more than the colour of the soil, 'tis intended to show the nature of it too, for they always apply it to a sandy soil of a reddish hue, interspersed, for the most part, with pieces of sandstone of the same colour, or somewhat deeper." *Morton.* p. 40.

RED-WELL. In Morton's time this was the designation usually given to a mineral spring. " A spring of this kind is here commonly known by the name of the *red-well,* or the *red water,*" &c.   p. 273.

RED-WIND. An easterly wind, to which the blight was formerly (and is still) attributed. *Morton*, p. 331.

REEVE, *n.* The female of the Ruff.

REEST, *n.* The skin of bacon. Harts.

RIBBLED, *s.* Wrinkled. "His forhead war *ribbled*."

RICK, *s.* To strain a joint. Bat.

RIDDLED, *s.* Reduced in pocket. "Amwust *riddled*."

RINGS, *n.* Thin partitions of stone found dividing layers of sand. *Morton*, p. 129.

RIN-SIEVE, *i. e.* reen-sieve. A very fine sieve. Dan. *reen*, purus. Ev. Bat. *ruyin-siv*.

RISS,
RIZ. } Rose. This form of the preterite is an archaism for which respectable authority may be adduced.

> "—— there, I *risse* ungently."
> *B. and F. Wit at several Weapons*, i. 1.
> "Did not you mark a woman my son *ris* to?"
> *B. and F. Hum. Lieut.* i. 1.

In *Jonson's Grammar* "*ris*, rise, or rose," are given as the *pret.* of to rise.

ROCK. This word is used by our quarriers in a slightly different sense to what is generally understood by the word. They apply it, as they did in Morton's time, to "a pile or parcel of any stone found disposed in strata." p. 265.

ROCK-SPRING. A lasting or perennial spring, "whose duct or channels are in the fissures or intervals of *rocks*."—*Morton*, p. 265.

ROMPS, *s.* "All a *romps*." In a confused state.

ROPE, *n.* *Pret.* of to reap. Often pron. *rup*.

ROUNCING. Roaring. "A *rouncing* fire." "A *rouncing* wind."

ROUT, *n.* A noise made by sheep. "There's another *rout* among they ship." Ic. *rauta*, mugire.

   2. To snore loudly. In *Barret's Dictionary*, 1580, ": a *routing* when one doth sleepe," is rendered *rhonchus.* A. S. *hrutan*, stertere.

ROYL, *s.* To sit awry. Bat.

   2. To reproach. " A's bin a *roylin* at ma arl day ;" perhaps a coarse pronunciation of *rail.* Ex. and For. *rile.*

RUCK, *n.* A heap. Clothes gathered together, or creased, are said to be " all in a *ruck.*" Car. Wilb. Hart. Sui. G. *ruka*, cumulus. Gael. *ruchd*, a rick.

RUDGE, *s.* A deep waggon-rut.

RUN. The "*grain*" of stone, the direction in which it most easily cleaves.

RUNNEL, *n.* A brook or small stream. A. S. *rin.* Ic. *rinna*, rivulus.

RUSH-BENT, *n.* A rush stalk.

RUSTY. Restive. "A *rusty* horse." Bat.

RYE-LAND, *n.* A species of soil similar to the red-land before described, so called from its fitness for that sort of grain.—*Morton*, p. 54. This does away with the difficulty of accounting for the frequent recurrence of rye-hills, rye-lands, &c., as names of fields, though within the memory of the oldest persons they have never been sown with that grain.

SAAT, } *s.* Soft. Dan. *sagte.* Germ. *zart.* Teut.
ZAAT, }   *saecht*, mollis. Ak. Bar. *sate.* Jen. *zat.*

SAAT-BREAD. Heavy bread, when it has not risen. Germ. *zähe*, tenacious, clammy.

SAD. Heavy, saturated with water. *Morton* informs us (p. 44) that "*clay*-land is called '*sad*-land' on the Thrapstone side." A road is said to be "*sad*" when, after much rain, its surface is muddy. A. S. *sadian*, saturare. Car. Tees.

SAG, *n.* To bend or give way from great pressure. Ic. *svegia*, flectere, curvare. Car. Tees. For. Ev.

SALLOWS. Bridges supposes this word to have been used to denote, not only a plantation of willows, but a wood or thicket of any kind of trees; hence Salcey Forest is termed in old records " *Foresta de Salceto.*" Vide *Hist. of Nothampt.* vol. ii. p. 256.

SAMELY, *n.* Similar, monotonous.

> " Oh *samely* naked leas! so bleak, so strange."
> *Clare's Vil. Min.* p. 58.

SARVER. A server, *i. e.* small basket to hold corn.

SCAUT, *s.* To strain with the feet in supporting a heavy weight. Ak.

2. To plough up the land in attempting to stop. Sui. G. *skiuta*, propellere. Her.

SCHOLARD, *s.* A scholar. " I ben't no *scholard*," is a phrase frequently in the mouth of a labouring man when addressed in terms which he cannot understand.

SCOFFLE. To scramble. "To *scoffle* a basket of apples," *i. e.* to throw them among a number of children that they may be scrambled for.

SCOTCH. To impede or stop a wheel, &c. Ev. Hart.

2. A supporter.

SCRASE. To scratch or graze. "These tiables be *scrased* allarmin." Dut. *krassen.* Germ. *kreitzen.*

SCRAT. To scratch. Car. Tees. Hart.

SCRATCHINS, *s.* The refuse of the "leaf" after the lard has been extracted. Harts. Ev.

SCRATCHWEED. Clivers. Morton.

SCRAUNCH, *s.* To crunch with the teeth. Teut. *schrantsen.* Bar.

SCRAWLIN. Thin and shrivelled : spoken of corn in the ear.

SCRIG, *n.* To strain. "Kain't ye *scrig* out another drop ?"

SCRINCH, *s.* A morsel. For. *scrimption.* "Not a *scrinch* left."

SCRIMMAGE. A fight or scuffle. Germ. *scrimen,* pugilare.

SCRINGE. To squeeze. A. S. *thringan.* For. Ev. Bar. *dringe.*

SCRUNGE, *s. Pret.* of the above. "A war so *scrunge.*"

SCULPS,
SCALPS, } *n.* Remains of turnips, &c. The hard portion from which the shoot proceeds, generally left by the sheep. Ic. *skalp,* vagina. Teut. *schelp,* putamen.

SEAM, *n.* Synonymous with crick ; a dry fissure or break in stone strata. A. S. *seam;* called also "a *dry joint.*"

SEBLET. A small basket to contain the seed-corn in sowing by broad-cast. A. S. *sad-leap,* a seed basket. Bat. For. Jen. *seed-lep.*

SEBLET-CAKE, *s.* A large seed-cake, with which farm-labourers are regaled at the end of the sowing season This, like all the other old farming customs, is fast growing obsolete. A custom somewhat similar prevails in Warwickshire, vide *Brand,* i. 217.

SECK. Second. " You go first, I'll be *seck.*"

SEMI-SIGHT, *s.* A child's plaything, consisting of flowers, &c., arranged under a piece of glass. A contraction of *See-my-sight.*

SEN, *n.* Self. "*Hirsen, hissen,*" M. Yorksh. Car. Bat.

> 2. *Pret.* of to say. "He *sen* so." Shaks. *Love's Labour's Lost,* iii. 1. In Shropshire used in the present tense. Hart. in *v.*

SESS, *n.* The upper part of the turf-layer, consisting of soft and friable earthy matter, not making such good fuel as the lower and harder formation.—*Morton.* Broc. has *soss,* anything foul or dirty. For. *suss,* an uncleanly mass. Harts. *soss,* do. Jen. *soss,* to throw a liquid from one vessel to another.

> 2. An invitation to a dog to eat. Broc. *sos.* For. *suss,* " an invitation to swine to come and eat their wash." The verb *soss,* to lap as a dog, occurs in Marshall's Yorkshire Glossary, Brochet, and the Teesdale and Craven dialects. Bat. *sus.* Jen. For. *soss,* a jumble or mess of food. *Soss,* " houndis mete." *Prompt. Parv.* Gael. *sos,* a mixture of food for dogs or swine. Teut. *sauss,* condimentum.

SESSO, *s.* A report of doubtful veracity, *i. e.* a *say-so.*

" I bean't zartin an't, mebby it's any a *sesso*." Compare, *say-so*, in the Herefordshire Glossary.

SET. A potato plant; the young quicks for hedges are also called "*sets*," or "*settins*." A. S. *set*.

SEVERAL. Frequently corrupted into *everhills*, *errils*, &c. A field or enclosure; originally a portion of common or fen land, assigned for a term to a particular proprietor, the other commoners leaving for the time their right of commonage. See *Hunter's New Illustrations of Shakespeare*, vol. i. p. 267. Shaks. *Love's Labour Lost*, ii. sc. 1.

> " He that holds lands or tenements in *severalty*, or is sole tenant thereof, is he that holds them in his own right only."
> *Blackstone's Commentaries*, b. ii. c. 12.

> " Of late he's broke into a *several*
> Which doth belong to me, and there he spoils
> Both corn and pasture."
> *Sir John Oldcastle*, iii. 1.

Old Fr. *sevrer*. It. *severare*, to separate.

SHACK, *n*. To shake. Car. Tees. A. S. *sceacan*. Teut. *shocken*.

2. To shed, as corn in harvest. Grose.

3. Loose grain usually given to the hogs. For.

SHACKLE, *s*. To escape or avoid: frequently applied to a person who flies from his bargain. A. S. *sceacan*.

SHACKLER. A low, idle, dishonest fellow. A. S. *sceacere*. Teut. *schække*, fur.

SHACKLETY. Loose, shaking. "A *shacklety* box."

When applied to a person it means worthless, dissolute. Teut. *schœckier-en*, alternare. Nearly allied to the verb *shack*, to idle, &c.; found in Ev. For. Hart. Bat.

SHALE, *n.* To cleave, as stones in being raised. *Morton*, p. 129. Like most of the words recorded by Morton, this term is still in use. A. S. *ascealian*. Teut. *schellen*, to peel.

SHALLOW. A scaly fish, in shape " betwixt a roach and a bream." *Morton*, p. 419. The *fin-scale* of Dr. Plot. *Nat. Hist. of Oxfordshire*, ch. vii. sec. 29.

SHUCK, *n.* A " *shuck*" of corn.

    2. *Pret.* of shake. " I war som *shuck.*" " I was some *shaken.*"

SIB, *n.* Relationship, kin. Teut. *sibbe.* A. S. *sib*, sanguinitas. A good old word used by Chaucer. Wilb. *B. and F. Two Noble Kinsmen*, i. 2.

SID. Seed. A. S. *sæd.*

SIDE, *s.* Space, width, side-room. " Give it plenty of *side.*" A. S. *sid, side*, latus, amplius, spatiosus.

SIDGROUND, *s.* A field newly laid to grass.

SIDLE, *n.* To walk side-ways; a winding footpath is also said to " *sidle.*"

SIGHT, *n.* A great number. " Theer were a gret *sight* of folks at our feast." Com. The shoemakers talk of having to do a great " *seet*" of work. Query " *seat*," or " *sight* ?"

SIKE, *n.* A spring or small stream. A. S. *sic.* Ic. *sijk.* In Cheshire, according to Wilbraham, a spring in a field, which, having no immediate outlet, forms a boggy place; which is, perhaps, a more correct

definition of the sense in which we use it. Car.
Lanc. Jam. Dr. Plot, in his *Natural History of
Staffordshire*, pp. 46, 47, describes many such springs.

SIKE, *n.* To cry, sob, or violently bewail. A. S.
sican, to sigh. Sui. G. *sikt*, a sigh. Hart. Ev.

> "*Sykinge* for my sennes."
> *Piers Ploughman*, p. 81.

SILE. To faint, to sink gradually.

> "They dig the grave deeper! your Nelly's beguil'd,
> She said, and she *siled* on the floor."
> *Clare's Poems*, 1820, p. 152.

SILT, *n.* A mixture of sand and mud left on land after
the subsiding of a flood. For.

SIMSO, *s.* A sham, unreal. "A *seem-so.*" On the
same principle as *sesso.* q. v.

SIN. Since. "It's a wic com Monday *sin* I seed you."
The old form of the word. Thus written by Chaucer
and other early writers.

SHANNY, *n.* Shame-faced. "How *shanny* a looks."
A. S. *shendan*, shame.

SHARD, *s.* A gap in a hedge. Ak.

SHARRIG,
SHEAR-HOG. } A yearling sheep when shorn. Ev.

SHAWNIN, *n.* Gathering sticks, &c., for fuel. A
farmer complained to me that the "village folks
were always *shawnin* on his land."

SHEED, *n.* To shed. "The corn has *sheeded.*" Ev.
A. S. *sceadan*, separare.

SHIFTY. Restless, changeable. Dan. *skifte*, mutare. Ev.

SHIP. Sheep, both singular and plural. Belg. *shæp.*
Harts.

SHOO. A word, when quickly repeated, used to drive away birds, &c. Wel. *siw*. Old Fr. *chou*. Germ. *sheuchen*, to drive away. Jam. *shue*.

> "*Shough, shough!* up to your coop peahen!"
> *B. and F. Maid in the Mill*, v. 1.

Cotgrave gives "*chou*, a voice wherewith we drive away pullein." This word appears common to the midland counties, and is found in most of the glossaries. It is also used in the sense of "to hasten," as "*shoo* along," *i. e.* hie away; and thus in the children's lines to the lady-bird, or, as it is here called, the "lady-lock"—

> "Lady-lock, lady-lock! *shoo* all the way home."

SHOGGLE. A slow trot; also used as a verb. Ev. *shog*. There is the Teut. *schockelen*, to shake.

SHOOL, *n.* To carry as a pretence: thus rendered in the glossary to Clare's Poems.

2. To skulk. "Did you notice how he *shooled* away?"

SHOON, *n.* Shoes. The old plural termination. "Some nouns (says Ben. Jonson), according to the different dialects of several parts of the country, have the plural of both declensions, as house, houses, housen; eye, eyes, eyen; *shooe, shooes, shooen.*"— *Works*, vol. ix. 302.

SHOUL. A shovel. Dut. *school*. Ak. Jen. Her. The syncopoted form of similar words is found in all dialects; thus *deil* for *devil* in the Northern; *nowl*, *navel*, in the East Anglian, &c.

SKAT, *s.* A shower of rain of short continuance.

There is a proverb at Kenton, in Devon, mentioned by Risdon—"When Halldown has a hat let Kenton beware of a *skat*." Sui. G. *skiuta*, jaculare.

SKEG, *s.* A fool or clownish fellow. A contraction or corruption of *suck-egg*, which is also used to express the same thing. "There is a nationality in districts as well as in countries," says Mr. Chambers, in his *Popular Rhymes of Scotland;* "nay, the people living on different sides of a streamlet, or of the same hill, sometimes entertain prejudices against each other not less virulent than those of the different sides of the British Channel, or Pyrenees." Many instances of this might be pointed out in Northamptonshire. The following couplet may be given without hazarding the charge of irrelavency, as it illustrates the use of the word :—

> " Brackley *skegs*
> Come t' Imly ta et th' addled eggs."

The above elegant effusion is addressed to any of the inhabitants of that ancient town who may chance to pay a visit to the neighbouring village of Evenly, *vulgo* Imly. Again, the men of Grendon go by the name of *moon-rakers*, in consequence, it is said, of a party of them having once seen the moon reflected in a pool, and attempted to draw it out by means of rakes, under the impression that it was a cheese !

SKEG. The wild damson.

SKERRY, *n.* A small boat, formerly much used in the fenny districts. In an old road-book Crowland is said to be " so remote from pasture that yᵉ inhabitants are obliged to goe a milking by water in little boats, called *skerrys*, which carry two or three persons at a time."—*Britannia Depicta, or Ogilby Improved*, 1724. Lat. *scaphula, scapha*. Goth. *veerje*.

SKEW, *s*. To shy, or start aside, as a cow at an object with which she is not familiar. In *Carew's List of Cornish Words*, "*skew*" is rendered "*shunne*." Dan. *skiev*, oblique. Teut. *schew*, timídus. Fr. *secourer*, to move violently.

SKIT, *s*. A piece of scandal, or ill-natured jest. Ic. *skætingr*, dicteria a cerba.

SKILE,
SKALE, *n*. To move off, to retract. "The keeper's comin, *skale* off." "You arn't goin to *skile* off that bargin." Metaphorically from the stone-masons' phrase, to "*scale* off;" from the A. S. *scylan*, separare, or the Sui. G. *sky*, vitare.

SKIMMER, *n*. A flat piece of wood to float on the surface of water carried in buckets, to prevent its spilling over from the oscillation of the bearer.

SKIN-FLINT. A mean, avaricious person. One who, as the proverb says, will

"*Skin a flint* worth a fardin,
Spwile a knife worth a grat" (groat).

The Eastern languages have the same expression. Abdalmalek, one of the Caliphs of the house of Ommiades, a prince noted for his extreme avarice, was surnamed "Raschal Hegiarah," literally "the skinner of a flint."

SKIP, *n*. A small basket. A. S. *scep*. Teea. Hart. Ev. Also a wooden utensil used in brewing. *Vide* LADE-SKIP.

H

SKIVVER, *s.* A skewer. Jen. Bar. Dan. *skove.*

SLAB-STONES. Broad and thin stones. Morton. Teut. *schlabbe.*

SLABBY. Muddy, miry. A word still retained in our dictionaries, though obsolete in composition. Dut. *slibbe,* limus. Gael. *slaibeach,* cænosus, lutosus.

SLADE, *s.* A valley; a field, the bottom of which is frequently so called. Mr. Halliwell says, *ap. e.,* " I have heard the term in Northamptonshire applied to a flat piece of grass, and to a border of grass round a ploughed field."

SLAG, *s.* Slack. " It's too tight; *slag* it." Bat. *slagur.* A. S. *sleac.*

SLAKE, *s.* To decompose, or wear away, as some species of stone when exposed to the weather. A. S. *aslacian.*

SLAN, *s.* A sloe. A. S. *slan.* Hart. Ak.

SLANG, *n.* A narrow slip of land. Hart. Ev.

SLAT, *s.* To split or crack. " I'll *slat* your head for ye, young un." A. S. Ak.

SLIBBER, *s.* To slip or miss one's footing. Dut. *slibberigh,* slippery.

SLINK, *n.* An abortive calf. Jam. Wilb. For.

2. To " cast," or bring forth prematurely, as a cow. Germ. *schlenken,* abjicere. Harts. has " *slink veal,* such calves as are killed when under some disorder."

> " The Germans loath to eate of a *slinke* (or young calfe cut out of the cowes belly before it be calved), but in princes courts, both in Italy and Spaine, it is accounted one of the daintiest dishes."
>
> *The Valley of Varietie.* Lond. 1638, p. 33.

SLIVE, *n.* To do anything slyly, to conceal or disguise.

2. To slip, or slide down. Her. Hart. Wilb. and Car. have *slither.*

SLIVER,
SLIVVER, } *n.* To split or slice. A. S. *slifan,* findere. For. Hart. Car. Wilb. either as verb or substantive.

SLOGET, *s.* A sloven; generally applied to a woman. Sw. *slodder.*

SLOGETY, *s.* Slovenly. "Her does her work so *slogety.*" Tees. *sloggering.* Belg. *slorig,* sordidus.

SLOMMACKIN. Large and clumsy. "A gret *slommackin* wench." Teut. *slommeringhe,* quisquiliæ. Hart.

SLOOMY, *n.* Dull and gloomy. "How *sloomy* a lucks." Teut. *sluymen,* leviter dormire.

SLOP-FROCK, *n.* A smock-frock. Clare. Forby derives it from the A. S. *slop,* stola.

SLOVE, *n. Pret.* of "*slive,*" or "*sliver.*"

SLUDDER,
SLUDGE, } *s.* Mud and dirt; more particularly applied to that which covers the roads after great rains. Teut. *slodderen,* flaccescere, &c. Ev. Tees. *sludge.* Hart. *slud.* Bat. *sludder.*

SLUG-A-BED. A sluggard.

"Why, lamb! why, lady! fie, you *slug-a-bed.*"
Romeo and Juliet, iv. 5.

SLUT-GRATE. The hearth grating, through which the ashes fall. Ev.

SMUG, *n.* To conceal or hide. "*Smug* the bottle under the rick." Dan. *smug*, clandestinus.

SNAT-BERRIES. The fruit of the yew-tree.

SNEAD, *s.* ⎞ The pole of a scythe. A. S. *snæd.* Bar.
SNEATH, *n.* ⎠ Jen. Ak. Tees. *sned.* Ev. *sneath.*

SNETHERUM, *s.* A sharp "cutting" fellow.

SNITHING, ⎞ Sharp and keen. "A *snithing* wind."
SNITHERIN. ⎠ A. S. *snidan*, to cut. Ev. *snithing.*

SNIG. To sneak. "How a *snig'd* away when a saw I." Dan. *sniger.*

SNIGGLE. A snail; also the shell. Goth. *snigill.* Sw. *snigel.* Dan. A. S. *snægl.*

SNIPE, *n.* An icicle. Ev. Dan. *snip*, the end or point of a thing. Germ. *schneppe*, a peak, from the root of *neb* (with the sense of shooting or thrusting, like a sharp point); hence the common name of the woodcock, "*snipe*," is derived from the same source, in consequence of its length of bill or "*nib.*"

SOCK, *n.* The boggy substratum of marshy soils. For. "*sock*, the superficial moisture of land not properly drained off." A. S. *socian*, macerare; *soc*, suctus.

SOCK-PIT, ⎫ A farm-yard drain, or hole, which forms
SOCK. ⎬ the receptacle of the drainage. Wel.
 ⎭ *soc*, a drain or sink.

SOKE. A patch of marshy land. Her. Harts. *sok*, the liquid manure which oozes from a dunghill. Ic. *sock*, mergor.

2. A long draught. "A good *soke*," *quasi* suck.

SOME. This word with us is used as an augmentative. Ex. "It war a wet day istray." "Aye, it war *some* wet." "He does *some* eat," *i. e.* is a great eater.

" It is *some* late." In some cases it sounds like an inversion of the ordinary termination. " The night's *some* dark," *i. e.* darksome. It is also used in the sense of " *thereabouts.*" " How far be it to the town ?" " Five mile, or *some.*" This agrees well with the Cornish and Devonian signification, as given by Carew in his Survey. " In conjecturing what number may effect a thing, they adde, ' or *some*,' as two or *some*, ten or *some*, twentie or *some*, *id est*, thereabouts."

SOME-DEAL. In some degree ; also a great many. Ex. " Was there many people at your feast ?" " Ees, theer war *some-deal* o' folk." A. S. *sum dœl.*

> " A good wif was ther of beside Bathe,
> But she was *som del* defe, and that was scathe."
> *Chaucer's Prologue to Cant. Tales.*

> " Whether the muse so wrought me from my byrth,
> Or I too much beleev'd my shepheard peeres,
> *Some dell* ybent to song and musickes mirth."
> *Spenser's Shep. Cal.* Dec. v. 40.

SOMETHING, *s.* Often used for somewhat. " *Something* cross." So *Shakespeare*—

> " But gentle lady Anne,
> To leave this keen encounter of our wits,
> And fall *something* into a lower method."
> *Rich. III.* sc. 2.

SOO, SUE. { A word addressed to a cow, to *soothe* her, in order that she may stand quietly to be milked. Wel. *suaw*, to lull to rest.

SOOP. A sup, drop, or small quantity. Ex. " A

few *soops* o' rain." Hart. has it in the sense of a draught.

SOODLE, *n.* To linger, to go reluctantly.

SOUL, *s.* A very common expletive. "A *soul* of a row." "A *soul* of a bad fellow."

SOWS, *s.* Woodlice.

SPALDER, *n.* To split wood. Her. *spill* and *spall.* Teut. *spulten*, separare.

SPICKET. A spigot, or peg to stop a faucit. Tees. *spiddick.*

SPIRE-GRASS, *n.* A tall species of sedge, growing on fenny land. *Discorse concerning the Drayning of Fennes*, 1629.

SPIT. The depth of a spade. Turf is divided into "*spits*," or depths. "One *spit*, two *spit*," &c. Dut. *spit.* For. Bar. Jen. Car. Her.

SPLARRADASH, *s.* Fine, excellent.

SPLIGHT. A word for which we have no equivalent in "National English :" it is applied to the state of a wound before coalescense. The word occurs in an old poaching song, a great favourite with our rustics, and an authority by no means to be discarded in such matters.

> "The very first night we had bad luck,
> My very best dog he soon got stuck :
> He came to me both bloody and lame,
> And sorry was I to see the same.
> > So fal, &c.

> "I search'd his wounds, and I found them *splight*;
> 'Says I, some keeper's done this out of spite,' &c."

Clearly the Dut. *splyte*, rend asunder. Teut. *spligten*. Dut. *splyten*, separare.

SPRACK, *s.* Lively, intelligent. " My boy's a *sprack* un." Ic. *spaca*. Wilb. *spact*. Her. Ak. Bar.

SPRAT, *n.* A variety of early barley. Morton.

SPRIT, *n.* A sprout ; the awn of barley. Teut. *spiet*.

SPROT. *Pret.* of to sprout.

SPULT, }
SPELT, } *s.* Brittle. Bat.

SQUAB-PIE, *s.* A pie made of a singular compound of meat and apples. " Cornwall *squat-pie*" is mentioned in *Dr. King's Art of Cookery*."

SQUEAM. The noise made by swine in a state of "*fret*," or restlessness.

SQUINE, *s.* To squint. " A *squines* shockin bad, don't a'." Bat. Ev. For. *squinny*.

SQUITCH. Couch grass. A. S. *cwice* (Somner.) Sw. *quicka*. Hart. *scutch*. Also pronounced *twitch*.

> " The ploughmen now along the doughy sloughs,
> Will often stop to clean their ploughs
> From teazing *twitch*, that in the spongy soil
> Clings round the coulter, interrupting toil."
> *Clare's Shep. Cal.* p. 29.

STACK. A mass "or bench" of stone in strata. In Pembrokeshire the insular rocks of the coast are locally termed " *stacks*."

2. A quantity : not always conveying the idea of a pile. " A *stack* a folks."

STADDLE. The stone posts which support a rick. A. S. *stæthol*, a support. To be found in Tusser and other early agricultural writers. Ak. Bar. Tees.

In the latter dialect applied to " the frame-work"
of the post.

STAFF. The spar or "*round*" of a chair, &c. Ev.
A. S. *staf*.

STAG. An old boar. Ic. *steggr*, the male of wild
beasts.

STAGGERS, *n.* A disease in cattle, sheep, &c., one of
the principal symptoms being a giddiness in the head.
Dut. *staggeren*, to reel, totter, &c.

> "*Staggers* is a loosiness in the head, breeding of
> cold and the yellows."
>
> *A Discourse to know the Age of a Horse.*
> Lond. 1810.

STAIRN (pron. *steayarn*). Stairs. "Goo up *steyearn*."

STALL. To founder, or become fixed, as a waggon in
a boggy road. Ev. Clare.

STAMMINLY, *n.* Profusely, excellently well. " The
beer was *stamminly*." " Old Gaffer Garlick's gwain
an *stamminly*." For. has *stam*, a matter of amazement.

STAM-WOOD, *n.* The roots of trees stubbed up.
Also a Rutlandshire provincialism. A. S. *stamne*,
a stump.

STANK, *n.* A dam across a stream. Ev. For. Her.
Also used as a verb, to *stank* a stream.

STARNEL, *s.* A starling. Ev. A. S. *stærn*. It.
stornello.

STARCH, *n.* Staunch. " He's a *starch* friend of
mine." I have only heard this word once, and that
in the phrase given. If not a corruption, which I
am inclined to believe, it is the A. S. *starc*, firmus.

STAR-SHOT,
STAR-JELLY,
STAR-FALLING,
} *n.* Masses of clear viscid and tenacious matter, often found in fields, or on the tops of hedges, &c., so called from its being supposed by the country people to fall from the stars. Morton (who is followed by Pennant) thus speculates as to its real formation:—"As to the origin of this body, it has, in many particulars, a near analogy with animal substances: it appears to me to be only the disgorge or casting of birds of three or four sorts; of those sort or fowl in particular that at certain seasons do feed very plentifully upon earth-worms, and the like."

"Amongst ourselves, when any such matter is found in the fields, the very countreymen cry, it fell from heav'n and the *starres;* and, as I remember, call it the spittle of the *starres.*"

White's Peripateticall Institutions, 1656, p. 148.

STATTY, *s.* A "*statute*" fair for hiring servants. *Plot's Oxfordshire.* Car.

STARVED. Cold. "I be so *starved.*" "It's a *starvin* wind." Ev.

STEER. Steep, abrupt. Germ. *steil,* abruptus. A. S.

stæger, gradus, ascensorium; from the verb *stigan*, ascendere.

2. To confuse with loud talking. Ev. In the Southern district to "*dinny.*" A. S. *styran.* Germ. *storen*, turbare. Gael. *stair*, noise, confusion.

STICK, STOCK, AND STONE. A proverbial phrase to éxpress a clear riddance. "Be they gone?" "Eez, sure, *stick, stock, and stone.*"

STINGE, *s.* (The *g* soft.) A sting. "*Stingein* nettles." A. S. *stincg.* Ak.

STOCK. To stop in growth. Some kinds of stone are said to be *stocked*, when, by exposure to the weather, they become indurated. Wheat, also, is said to be *stocked* when its growth has been checked by an analogous cause. "After much wet a very hot day will occasion a sudden alteration in the colour of corn; and the corn that is thus discoloured is usually *stocked*, as the husbandmen call it; that is, it does not come up to the height and perfection of the rest that escapes this injury."—*Morton.* To "*stock*" trees or shrubs, to dig them up by the roots. Ev. has "*stocked*, stopped in growth." Germ. *stocken*, to stop, stanch, or stagnate. Gael. *stocaich*, torpesce.

STOCKINS. Land reclaimed from the woods; from *stock*, to fell timber. In the neighbourhood of Whittlebury it is frequently found as the name of a field originally cleared from the forest. Germ. *stock-raum.*

STODGED, *n.* Distended; filled to the "*stretch*," as a cow's udder with milk. We have, also, in a similar sense, "*stodgeful*," and "*stogdy.*" For. has

" *stodge*, to stir up various ingredients into a thick mess." Ev. *stodge*, full. Car. Hart. Moor, *stodjy*, clogsome.

STONE-BATCH, *n.* A hard species of clay. *Morton*, p. 95. Wel. *baich*, a burden.

STONE-WATER. A petrifying spring, of which there are severnl in this county. A good and expressive combination. "These waters are apply'd to by many of our countrymen for curing the fluxes of their cattel, which they commonly stop, with twice or thrice drinking."—*Morton*, p. 272.

STOOL. A cluster of rushes. *Morton*, 154. *Marshall*, in the Glossary appended to his *Rural Economy of the Midland Counties*, has the word " *stool*, to ramify, as corn."

STOUT, *s.* Proud. "Madam looked quite *stout* to-day." Teut. *stolte*, superbus. Sui. G. *stolt*. Ic. *stolltar*, magnificus, fastosus.

STOVE,
STOVEN, } *n.* A stump of a tree. Ev. *stovin*. The same term is also given to a young shoot from the stump, after the trunk has been felled.

STRAM-OUT, *n.* To stretch. Dan. *strammer*. Hence, also, " *strammer*," a great lie.

STREEK, *n.* To stretch out. A. S. *streccan*. Jam. Tees. *streak*. The *pret.* of this word is *strock*.

STRET. Deficient, *straitened* " We are so *strett* for water." Ev.

STRET-FINGER'D, *s.* Honest. A quaint expression.

STRIKE, *n.* A bushel. See *Brand's Popular Antiquities*, iii. p. 211.

STRIT, *s.* A street. The roads of a village are always thus designated. A. S. *strœt.*

STROCKLE, STRICKLE. { The round piece of wood used for *striking* off the overplus grain from a *strike* or bushel. In Staffordshire, *strickless. Shaw's Staffordshire,* vol. ii. p. 20. Teut. *strecklen,* leviter tangere. Germ. *streich-holz.*

STROMP, *s.* To tread heavily. Germ. *strampfen.* " I yard un *strompen* down steyearn."

STRUTTLE, *n.* The stickleback, a small fish found in brooks. For. *stuttle.*

STUBS, *s.* Rotten and decayed roots ; also the rough points of recently cut hedges, &c. *Vide* Hart. Jam. *stols.* A. S. *stub.*

STUBBY. Prickly, full of " *stubs.*" Gael. *stobach.*

2. Small. " That's a *stubby* child." Sw. *stubig,* brevis.

STULP, *n.* The stump of a tree.

> " The woodman's robin startles coy ;
> Nor longer to his elbow comes,
> To peck with hunger's eager joy,
> 'Mong mossy *stulps,* the littered crumbs."
> *Clare's Shep. Cal.* p. 24.

For. defines it, " a short post, put down to mark a boundary," &c. *Stoop,* or *stoup* (with the customary omission of the *l*) is the pronunciation which obtains in the more Northern and Eastern counties. M. Yorks. Lanc. Moor, Jam. Tees. Car. Ray derives it from the Lat. *stupa.* Our form most nearly resembles the Sui. G. *stolpe.*

STY. A little boil or tumor on the edge of the eyelid. Broc. Moor. For. *stiony*, which he derives from the Gk. ὄπιον, from its hardness.

SUCK, *s.* A name given to any watery drink, more particularly applied to small beer. Wel. *sucan.* Hence the proverb—

"Gwell *sucan meziant nogwin* curdawd."

Better is small beer that is one's own, than wine on charity.

SUCK, } The cuckoo; also applied to a stupid
SUCK-EGG. } fellow. Similar to the Scotch *gowk.*

SUCK. A word used to call sheep, &c. In Hallam-shire *sic* is the word used to call pigs. A. S. *sic*, a pig. Gael. *siuc*, vox quâ equi compellantur.

SUCK-BOTTLE. The common white flowering nettle.

SUCKLERS. *n.* Slips of willow, &c., used for planting. Morton.

SUCH, *n.* Used for such-like. A keeper complained that all sorts of " varmint" infested his woods, " pole-cats, wizzles, stoats, and *such.*" This appears to be the sense in which it is used in Leicestershire. Ev. in *v.*

SUDGED, *s.* Soaked. " He got well *sudged* in the storm." A. S. *socian.*

SUDS, *n.* Floods. Water mixed with sand and mud; formerly applied to the waters of the fens.

"To be surrounded, or lye in the *suds*, as we say, three quarters or halfe a yeere, more or less, doth mischiefe, not helpe the ground."
Discourse concerning the Drayning of Fennes, 1629.

In all probability the phrase, "to be in the *suds*," *i. e.* difficulties, took its rise from this source.

SUGGLE, *s.* To cuddle.

SUMMET, *s.* Something; a contraction of somewhat.

SUNDAY-MOON, *s.* There is a pretty generally received idea that a new moon on a Sunday will bring a flood before it is out. Thus the proverb, "*Sunday's moon* floods 'for'ts out."

SURBED, *n.* To "*surbed*" a stone is to invert it, to place it in an opposite position to what it held in the earth. The term is mentioned in *Plot's Oxfordshire* as applied in a similar manner to coal. Morton. Fr. *sur.* A. S. *beddian*, sternere.

SURRY. Sorry, in bad plight. "A *surry* mare." Ev.

SUTHER, *n.* To sigh heavily. "She geunne such a *suther* an then siled on the floor."

SWASHE, *n.* Hog's wash. *Whash* is the Northern pronunciation of *wash.* Wicliffe writes *waisch.*

SWALE, *n.* The shade. For. Clare. A. S. *scua.*
2. To melt or consume without flame; in S. Hants. *swelter. q. v.* Ev. Broc.

SWALY. Shady. "A *swaly* bank."

SWALLOW-HOLES, *n.* "Chinks or little chasms in the surface of the earth," so called from their "*swallowing*" up the waters of small streams, &c. Morton. Sw. *swall.* Teut. *schwal*, inundatio.

SWANKEY, *s.* Small-beer. West.

SWARM, *n.* To climb up a tree by clasping it with the arms and legs. Bat. Car. Tees. Ev. For.

SWAT, *s.* To sweat. A. S. *swat.* Hart.

2. The fermentation of corn in the stack.

> " In these monthes is good to thrashe forth cornne
> after it hath bade a goode *sweate* in the mowe, and
> so dried againe."
>
> *Order and Government of a Nobleman's House,*
> 1606. Arch. xiii. p. 383.

SWEG. To sway up and down. Hal. gives this as a
Lincolnshire word. Hart. *swagle.* Ic. *sweigia.* Sui.
G. *swiga.*

SWELT,
SWELTER. { To overpower with heat. "Enow to *swelt* un to death." "*Sweltin* hot," &c. A. S. *swylt,* swælan ? Ic. *swæla,* suffocare. Germ. *schwelen,* to consume slowly. Her. For. Pal. Broc.

2. To consume without flame. Ak. *v. swilter.*

SWIG. To drink. Ak. Bar. Hart. Ic. *swiga.*

SWINGE, *n.* To singe. Her. Car. Hart. Also a
word of that very numerous class expressive of casti-
gation. From the A. S. *swingan,* flagellare.

SWINGEL, *s.*
SWIPPLE, *n.* { That part of a flail, or "thrail," which "*swings.*" For. Ev. *swipple.* Hart. *swepple.* A. S. *swinge,* fla-gellum.

SWITHIN, ST. Rain on this day is looked upon as
presaging a good crop of apples. The saint is then
said to be christening his fruit. I cannot find any
incident in the life of this saint which will serve to
hang a conjecture on.

TABBER, *n.* To tap or pat, so as to make a sound.
Ev.

TACKLE, *s.* Agricultural implements, harness, &c. Ak.

TAG, *s.* Second. "To pulle *tag*," *i. e.* to be the second puller.

TAILBOARD. A board inserted in the hind part of a cart.

TAILINS. Tail-ends. The refuse corn, generally given to the poultry. Bar. Ak. Ev.

TAM,
TOMMY, } *s.* Bread, meat, or any food requiring mastication, opposed to broth, porridge, &c. The Wel. *tama* has exactly the same meaning.

TAMMY-BAG, *s.* A provision bag.

TANK. A hard blow. "A *tank* on the head." Ev.

TAT. A child's game on the slate, similar to the "*kit-cat-carrio*" of *Moor*, p. 200.

TAY. Tea: words of a similar form, pea, flea, &c., are invariably thus pronounced. Till within the last few years there might still be found people who resisted the encroachment of this "*thin drink*," as they termed it, and manfully stuck to the more substantial beverage. The grandmother of an old lady still living recollected the first introduction of tea into the village in which she lived. A farmer of the parish had a friend in town, who, wishing to make some return for the various country commodities which he was in the habit of receiving, thought nothing would be so great a novelty as a pound of tea, at that time an article of luxury in London itself. Accordingly the tea was sent, and duly received. Never having seen or heard of the article before, the worthy couple were sorely puzzled to know how to use it; and, after many sage consultations, it was boiled with the bacon in lieu of cabbage. As may be readily imagined the unsavoury compound was not finished without many wry faces and execrations; and it is almost needless to add, the "new-fangled stuff" never afterwards formed a portion of their fare.

TAZZ. A rough head of hair. Ev. Dut. *tassen*, to heap up.

TEARY, *n.* Sticky. "The dressen them ship's made my hands *teary*." Ev.

TED, *s.* To spread abroad the new-mown hay. A. S. *tedrian*, tenerescere. Wel. *teddu*, lacerare.

TEDDER, *n.* To perplex or tease. "Don't *tedder* me." Sui. G. *tudda*, intricare.

TEEM, *n.* To pour out. A word common to all the Northern and Anglian counties. Car. For. Tees. Ic. *taema*, vacuare.

TELL'D, *n.* Did tell. Tees.

TERRY, *s.* To provoke or torment. A. S. *terian*. For. *terrify*.

TEW, *s.* A quantity or crowd. "Such a *tew* of sheep." Allied, probably, to the Teut. *touwen*, premere pressare.

THACK, THEEK, *s.* Thatch; and as a verb, *to thatch*. A. S. *thac, theccan*. Ic. *thikia*. For. Car. Tees. Jam. Ev. The constant use of this word, and that of dike (A. S. *dic*), has given rise to the proverb—

"*Thack* and dyke,
Northamptonshire like."

I

THACK-SPARROW. The common house-sparrow; so called from its building in the thatch. Ev.

THERD-BAROW. A tithing man; formerly so al led in Northamptonshire, but now obsolete. Vide *Norden's Delineations of Northamptonshire*, 1720, p. 37.

THILL. The shaft of a waggon or cart. *Troilus and Cressida*, iii. 2.

THONE. Corn too soft for grinding is said to be "*thone;*" damp, moist weather is also termed "*thoney.*" It is most likely, as Dr. Evans conjectures, the old *pret.* of the A. S. *thawen*, regelari.

THOU. Traces may still be observed among the old, of the ancient etiquette which prescribed the use of this pronoun to an equal or inferior, reserving the plural *you* for addressing superiors. *Marshall*, in his *Yorkshire Glossary*, has recorded a similar custom. "The farmers of the Eastern Moorlands '*thou*' their servants; the inferior class, (and the lower class of men in general,) frequently their wives, and always their children. These distinctions are sometimes the cause of awkwardness: to '*you*' a man may be making too familiar with him; while to '*thou*' him might affront him." A curious collection of similar peculiarities in other languages will be found in the *Battledore of George Fox*. Lond. 1660. This illustrates the passage in *Twelfth Night*, act iii. sc. 2.

> "Taunt him with the licence of ink; if thou *thou'st* him some thrice it shall not be amiss."

THRAIL, *s.* A flail. North. Beds. Bat. A. S. *threscol.* Sp. *trilla.*

THROV. *Pret.* of to thrive.

THRUP. This is invariably the pronunciation of the A. S. *thorp*, a village. Thus Chaucer—

> "*Thropes* and bernes, shepenes and dairies."
>
> *Wife of Bath's Tale.*

When in composition with some other word the *th* becomes *t*: thus *Rothersthorpe* is called *Ros'trup; Abthorpe, A'trup.*

THUNDER-BOLT. A belemnite, vulgarly supposed to fall from the skies.

THURROW, *n.* A furrow. Ev.

THWITTLE, *n.* To whittle, cut, make white by cutting. Ray. A. S. *thwitan.*

> "*Thwyting* is properly the cutting of little chippes from a stick."
>
> *Carew's Survey of Cornwall.*

Car. Tees. *white.* Hart. *thwite.*

TIDDY. Tender, weak, or puny; spoken of a lamb or young child. A. S. *tydr.*

TILL, *n.* Than. "He's better *till* me." Hart. Car.

TILTH, *n.* A ploughing. "That piece must have a fresh *tilth* over." "In good *tilth*," *i. e.* in good farming order. *Lewis*, in the Glossary contained in his *History of the Isle of Tenet*, gives "*tilt*, a ploughing or husbandlike order."

TIND, TEEND. { To light. "*Teend* the fire." A. S. *tendan.* Dan. *tende.* Ic. *tendra.* Wilb. Hart. &c. Ak. *tine.*

TINE, *s.* To divide or inclose a field, &c. A. S. *tynan.* Dut. *tuynen.* Ak.

2. A prong of a fork, harrow, &c. Her. Wilb.

TINNEY, *s.* Little, small Wel. *tim,* parvus. *Tinsy,* the more common form of the word, is far from being peculiar to this county.

TINT, *n.* A contraction of *it is not.*

TIT, }
TID. } A teat. A. S. *tit.* Ak. (1)

TIT, *s.* A cat. Wel. *titw.*

TOADLY. Gentle. " A *toadly* cow." Contraction of *towardly.* Ev.

TODGE, *s.* Thick spoon-meat. Mr. Ak. gives the A. S. *to-gereorde,* a taking to food or refreshing. Hart. *stodge.* Moor, *stodgey.*

TOLTER, *n.* To hobble. A. S. *tealtian.*

TOLTERING. Walking unevenly, or riding ungracefully. " He's a bad rider, a' goes so *toltering*-like."

TOMODGE. The ventricle of a pig. ⁚

TOOK. " I *took* him sich a flick o' th' yead," *i. e.* gave him.

TOOK-TO, *s.* Deceived, took in. " A's got *took-to* finely with them ship a bote this marnin."

TOOT, }
TOOTLE, } *n.* To play on the flute, to whistle; also applied to the singing of birds. Dut. *tuyten,* strepere.

2. To pry or poke about. C. " *tout,* to look out sharp." A. S. *totian,* eminere tanquam cornu in fronte.

TOPSY-TURVY MOSES WEBSTER. A phrase frequently applied to things in a state of disorder. It would appear to be a mere local allusion; but personality in old proverbs is not always a proof of their being localisms. Thus *Wilbraham*, in his *Cheshire Glossary*, records the phrase, " As fine as Dick's hatband ;" to which he adds, "this must be very local." The saying, however, is well known in this county, as well as Shropshire. Hart. in *v*.

TOT. A small mug. Teut. *tuyte*, cirnea. Dut. *tuyte*, a sucking bottle. Hart. Ev.

2. To pour out into *tots*; and hence frequently applied in a more general sense, to pouring from one vessel to another with a steady, careful motion.

TOTTER-GRASS. The name given to the *Briza media* in the Northern district.

TOWN. Every village, however small, boasts this appellation. The A. S. *tun* by no means conveys the idea of a large place.

TO-YEAR. This year. " A good crop *to-year :*" in the same manner as " *to-day*," &c. Bat. Bar.

TRAMP. A mendicant. Applied to any suspicious-looking personage who is on the " *tramp*." Ak. Car. Tees. Bar.

TRIG, *n*. Neat, trim. *Ben Jonson*, in the *Alchemist*, iv. 1, uses it in the sense of a coxcomb. Jam. Broc. Tees.

TRIVENT, *s*. A truant. Ev. *trivant*.

> " An asse, a trifler, a *trivant*."
> *Burton's Anatomy of Melancholy*, p. 10.

TROLLY-MOG. A dirty, slovenly female. Teut. *drollen*. Ic. *trulla*.

TROUNCE, *s.* To beat or chastise severely. Old Fr. *troncir.* Tees. For.

TRUNDLE. "You must take your *trundle*," i. e. chance or luck.

> " I've brought ye up, expect no more from me,
>   So take your *trundle*, and good luck may ye see."
>   *Vil. Min.* i. p. 41.

Most probably a figurative expression, from the A. S. *trendan*, anything turned or turning.

TUN-BOWL. *s.* A carrying tub used in brewing.

TUNNEL, *s.* A funnel. A. S. *tænel.*

TURF-BASS, *n.* A variety of rush, growing in damp places. Belg. *bies*, juncus.

TUSK, *s.* A tuft of grass or weeds. Wel. *tuwo.* Ev. *tussock.*

TUT. Offence. "To take *tut.*" Ev.

TUTTY. Cross, irritable. Bat. Ev. Jamieson has *titty*, a Renfrewshire word for " *testy*, ill-humoured." For. *tutter*, trouble.

TUZZLE, *s.* A sharp contest. Jen. Bar. Car. Germ. *tusselen*, to beat.

TWARD'N, *s.* It was not; a compound of three words, "*it war not:*" here, as Mr. Jennings has remarked, the *t* is not only converted into the *d*, but instead of being placed after the *n*, as analogy requires, it is placed before it, no doubt for the sake of euphony.

TWILLY-WILLY, *n.* Woollen or gown stuff. For. *twill.*

TWIN-FRUIT, *n.* Double fruit.

TWISTY. Contentious, ill-humoured.   Dut. *twistigh*.

TWIT, *s*. To reproach or hint a fault.   Bat.

> "The other rude termes, wherewith Devon and Cornish men are often *twyted*, may plead in their defence not only the prescription of antiquitie, but also the title of proprietie."
>
> *Carew's Survey of Cornwall*.

TWOADY. Disagreeable, loathsome, *i. e.* "*toady*." Her.   A very common term in the vituperative vocabulary.

> "As loathsome as a toad."
>
> *Titus Andronicus*, iv. 2.

UGGIN-WOY. Hither way, *i. e.* towards the driver. Addressed to a horse or plough-ox·   The Salopian Glossarist conjectures it to be formed by elision from "*come over again ;*" in *v. come hether.*

ULLAPSE! *s*. An exclamation when anything goes wrong.

UNDER-ONE. At once, together.   "You must du't all *under-one*."

UNEMPT. To empty.   Bat.

UNKED, HUNKID, *s*. Lonely, dull, miserable.   "I war so *unked* when ye war away."   "A *unked* house," &c.   Mr. Bosworth gives as the derivative the A. S. *uncyd*, solitary, without speech. Ak. Broc. Car. Ev. (Bat. *ungkid*.) Hart.

UPSETS, *s*. Blocks of iron, &c., used in ovens to keep the bread *up*.

UPSIDES. Even. "I'll be *upsides* with you, old boy." Wilb. Bar. Jen.

URK. A small child, or diminutive person. Fairies were formerly called "*urchins* ;" hence, perhaps, the appellation in the present instance.

US. We. " *Us* did, did'n *us* ?" we did, did we not. Occasionally used still more barbarously for ours. " We had *us* dinners." Ev. (2)

UZZARD, *s.* The letter *z*. A corruption of *z hard*. Ak. *izzard*.

VALLY. Value. A common vulgarism.

VAST, *s.* A vast number or quantity. " That field ull tiake a *vast* a' muck."

WALL. The outside of a rick, or the side of a layer of stone.

WALTON'S CALF, *s.* " As wise as *Walton's calf*," who, as the proverb goes on to inform us, " ran nine mile to suck a bull."

> "As the Hob, of Hornechurche, who, having never sene London before, nor London sene hym, in hys Christmas sute, sente to Bartholomewe faire, entering at White Chappel, buyes nothing but gaping seede, persuaded that as he is delighted to gaze, so others omitte not to loke on hym, wherby it is night ere he cometh to Aldergate, and so, as wise as *Walton's calf*, is fayne to returne home more foole than he came, for spending of horse-meat."
>
> *Arthur Hall's Works*, p. 106.

WAPSE, *s.* A wasp. A. S. *wæps*. We have a

similar transposition in the case of *hapse*. A. S. *hæpe*, an hasp. Ak. Bar. &c. For.

WAR-HOC! *s.* A word of warning, intimating that the person to whom it is spoken must move out of the way. A. S. *war*, aware. Jen. and Car. give the interjection " *war !*" beware.

WARK, *s.* To banter. A. S. *warc*, pain. Bat. *wurk*.

WARNT, } *s.* Warrant. "A wunt du't, I tell thee."
WARND, } "A wunt, wunt a ; I *warnd* as how a ull."

WARP, *n.* A mixture of fine sand and mud left on meadow-land after the receding of floods. Not peculiar to this county.

WASTRELS, *n.* A term applied to any waste or imperfect articles, as " *wastrel* bricks," &c. M.

WASTY. Consumptive. Ev. A. S. *westan*, vastare. " Maester R. looks martal *wasty*."

WATER-BLOBS, *n.* The meadow bught, or marsh marigold. Clare.

WATSHED. Wet in the feet, " *wet-shod*." Common, with slight variations, to all the English dialects.

WEER, } *n.* Our. " Les ha' *weer* baver," *i. e.* let us
WE, } have, &c. Ev. Car.

WELLICK. To beat or thrash. " You shall have a *wellickin*, my lad !"

WELLICKER. A hard blow.

WELLY, *n.* Well nigh. " *Welly* killed." Wilb. Hart. Car. Lanc. Bat. Ev.

WELT. A seam or fissure. Morton.

WEST, *s.* A sore place on the edge of the eyelid. *See* STY.

WHANG. To throw or "bang" with violence. Clare. Ev.

WHEAT-HOVEL-DAY, *n.* The day on which harvest is concluded, and the corn safely "*hovelled.*" A term, like the custom from whence it derives its origin, now fast becoming obsolete.

WHINGELIN. Peevish, touchy, as a child in bad health. Ev.

WHITALL,
WHITTAW. } A village saddler, or worker in leather; sometimes called a "*knacker.*" A. S. *hwit-tawere.* Bat. Ev. *whit-taw.*

WHOOLE, *n.* The weovil; the *Yule* of S. Hants.

WIC, *s.* A week. A. S. *wic.* The word, with us, passes unchanged into the plural. "It wants ten *wic* a Monday to weer fe-ast."

WILD, *s.* While. "A long *wild.*"

WILKS, *s.* "As cross as old *Wilks.*" With the exception of this record of his irritability, this gent has passed into utter oblivion.

WILL-GILL, *n.* An hermaphrodite. Common to most of the Anglian dialects. Mr. Hartshorne gives the Ic. *veill,* male compactus; *gil,* hiatus.

WILT,
WILTER, } *s.* To wither or dry up. Bat. has "*wilkt,* withered," a form of the *pret.* also current here.

WIMBLE-STRAW. *Cynosurus cristatus,* Linn. A. S. *windel-streowe.* Tees. Car. &c. in *winnel* and *windel-straw.*

WIND-ROWS. Hay raked together in rows that the

wind may dry it.   A. S. *windwian*, ventilare.   For.
Tees. Hart.   Broc. " *win*, to dry hay by exposing
it to the air."

WINDING-BELL. A bell tolled during the time of a
dead person being put into his shroud.   This was
formerly the case at King's Cliffe.   Vide *Bridges*,
vol. i. p. 432.

WINNOCK. To cry as a child.   A. S. *wanian*.   Sw.
hwina.   Teut. *weeken*.   Hart. *whinach*.   Bat. *winuk*.

WINTER-MEW. A bird of the gull kind.   Morton.

WIP. On one side. "Skew-*wip*."   Hart. *skeaw-whift*.

WIST, *n.* A small wicker basket used in brewing, in
order to prevent the malt from running through the
fosset.

WITCHEN. The quicken-tree, a species of wild ash.
Clare.

WITCHLIN, *s.* Unsteady, shaking.   A. S. *wicelian*,
movere, vacillare.   Dut. *wicken*, vibrare.   Gael. *uidel-
ach*, tottering.

WITCH-MEN, *n.* Guisers who go about on Plough-
Monday with their faces darkened, &c., similar to
the mummers of S. Hants.   *Forby*, under *Kitty-
witch*, describes a Yarmouth custom somewhat
similar.

PLOUGH-WITCH-
WITCH-   } MONDAY, *n.* Plough Monday.   The following paragraph from the *Northampton Herald*, of January 15th, 1848, will show how
fast the old customs peculiar to this day are becoming obsolete :—

"The ancient practice of 'plough-boys,' decked
with ribands, and daubed with paint, visiting the
neighbouring towns to collect pence for a holiday,
is fast falling into desuetude. On Monday last, a
few visited us, serving to remind us of the recurrence of the day; but they were unaccompanied
by the paraphernalia of exhibition which attracted
attention, and excited interest in our boyish days.
We are afraid the poor fellows obtained little beyond
the hootings and peltings of a mischief-loving youth-
ful mob."

WIZZEN'D. The *past pret.* of the verb *wizzen*,
not yet obsolete in the more Northern counties.
Withered, dried, or shrunk up. A. S. *wisnian*. Ic.
visn-a, arescere.

WOOD-LAND. "A hollow, fuzzy, black earth."—
Morton.

WOOD-SEERS, *n.* "Insects that lie in little white
knots of spittle on the backs of leaves and flowers.
How they come I don't know, but they are always
seen plentiful in moist weather, and are one of the
shepherd's weather-glasses. When the head of the
insect is seen turned upwards, it is said to betoken
fine weather; when downward, on the contrary,
wet may be expected."—*Clare's Vil. Min.* 211.

WOOT,
HOOT,
s. A term used to a horse when he is required to turn from the driver; opposed to OR. The word is sometimes
shortened into *hutt* or *woutt*, in which
form we find it in *Randolph's Muses'
Looking Glass.*

"If he can cry hy, ho, gee, *hut*, gee ho, it is better
I trow than being a boet."

Act iv. sc. 4.

In this play the writer makes his clown, Agroicus,
speak a Western dialect, mixed, however, with some
midland peculiarities.   Randolph was a native of
Northamptonshire, and his early days were spent in
a manner which must have familiarized him with the
language of his rustic neighbours.   The dialectal
medley which he has put in the mouth of Agroicus is
still characteristic of the neighbourhood of his birth-
place.

WORLD, *s*. A long space of time, an age.   " It 'l be
a *world* afore he's back."   A. S *woruld*, seculum.
Still retained in this sense in the last phrase of the
general doxology, " world without end."

WUNG, ⎫ A very common name for a field.   A. S.
WONG. ⎭ *wong*.   Ev. For.

WYND, *n*. A winch.   M.

YACK, *s*. A hard blow.   " A *yack* i' th' head."

YACKER, *s*. An acre.   Fields, also, of much larger
extent than an acre are called by this name, generally
in composition with some other word, as Green's
yacker, Rush-*yacre*, &c.   A. S. *accre*.

YAPNY, *s*. Half-penny.   Compare the Northern
hawpenny.

YARBS, *s*. Herbs.   Her.

YARN, *s*. To earn.   " I kaint *yarn* a penny."   Hart.
arn.   Germ. *arnen*.

2. *Pret.* of the verb to hear, *pro. year.* Ex. "I *yarn* as how you left bwuth them plazen." *En* was the ancient termination of the perfect tense, which would make it, in the way it is here pronounced, *yearen*, whence the change is easy.

YARD-BAND, or Tailor's yard-band. The three stars in the belt of Orion.

YAR-TELL, *i. e.* Heard tell. "I nar *yar-tell* a zitch a thin."

YATE, *s.* Same as HEIT. *q. v.*

YAWPIN, *n.* Loud talking. Ev. in *yorp.*

YEABLE, *s.* Able.

YEANDERS. Yonder. "*Yeanders* hill."

YEL-HUS. An ale-house.

YELLOWS. Dyer's weed. M.

YELM. A parcel of straw ready to be used for thatching. Bat.

YEO. Ewe. A. S. *eowe.* Belg. *ouwe.* Car. For. Tees. Ex.

YEPPURN. An apron. Ak. In Shropshire *apparn*, which Mr. Hartshorne derives from the Armoric.

YERNEST. Earnest-money, given by the hirer to bind an engagement.

YET, *s.* To hate. An instance of the very common substitution of the *y* for the aspirate.

YET-AS, }
YETTUS. } As yet. "I arn't bin *yet-as*." Ev. Bat.

YOICKS, BOB! A familiar exclamation of wonder or surprise. It occurs in an old Northamptonshire

ballad, which the compiler "booked" from oral re-
citation :—

> "I went into my che-amber to zee what I cud zee,
>   An there I saw cwots hangin up, one, two, and
>   three :
>   I went unto my lovin wife, to know how they
>   cam there
>   Wi'out the lafe o' me.
>   'Ya old fool! ya blind fool! why, kaint ye very
>   well zee,
>   They are three blankets ya mudder sent to me.'
>   *Yoicks, Bob!* an that's fun, blankets wi' boottons
>   on!
>   The loike I nivver see," &c.

The Northamptonshire song bears a curious resemblance to the Scotch ballad, "*Hame came our gude
man at e'en.*"

YORSHAR. To *Yorshar,* or "come Yorkshire" over
a person.   To defraud by means of some well-con-
certed stratagem.   The proverbial over-reaching
character of the Yorkshiremen has given rise to
phrases of the like import throughout the kingdom,
more particularly in those counties which, like
Northamptonshire, are within the ordinary circuit of
their dealings.

> "*Yorshar,* to put Yorkshire to a man is to trick or
> deceive him."
>
> *Lancashire Dialect,* 1757.

> Yorks. "I am a Yorkshireman born and bred, I
>   care not who knowes it : I hope true Yorkshire
>   never denies his county."

Scot. "I thought you looked like a subtle blade."

*A Brief and Witty Dialogue between a Yorkshire
and a Scottish man.* Lond. 1650.

YOWKIN. Yelping. "How they dug's be *yowkin*."

YILT, *s.*
GILT, *n.* { A young sow which has not yet had pigs.
Ak. A. S. *gilde*. Dan. *gylt*. Ev.
Hart. *gilt*.

PART II.

—

FOLK-LORE.

K

FOLK-LORE.

FAIRY-FOLK.

"Fairies black, gray, green, and white."
SHAKESPEARE.

THE belief in fairies, the most poetical of all our popular superstitions, still lingers among the rural population of Northamptonshire and South Warwickshire. That knavish sprite, Will-with-the-Wisp, or, as we call him, "Jinn with the burnt tail," still, as in the days of Shakespeare—

"Misleads night wanderers, laughing at their harm."

The hell-hounds, and their ghostly huntsman, are still heard careering along the gloomy avenues of Whittlebury; and tales of elfin deeds in "auld lang syne" yet constitute a leading feature of the winter's evening hearth-talk. It is almost unnecessary to add that the faith is in its last stage of decay. Sunday-schools have proved more potent exorcists than the "holy frercs," to whom Chaucer attributed their expulsion; and the fairies, like all other relics of old-world times, are fast following the bygone days of agricultural simplicity.

Steam-threshing machines have long superseded the
magic flail of the drudging goblin ; and even the danc-
ing-grounds of Queen Mab and her tiny lieges are
menaced by the sacrilegious coulters of patent ploughs.
The few gleanings which the most industrious researches
have enabled us to collect, are arranged in the following
notes, and the original narrations have, in all cases,
been strictly adhered to.

The traditions of the Northamptonshire peasantry
concerning the elves, or fairies proper, of the popular
creed, do not differ from those current in other parts of
the kingdom, and are in all respects conformable to the
mythological system preserved in the writings of the
Elizabethian dramatists. They are believed to be diminutive in stature, and in their dealings with mankind
exhibit the same mixture of good and evil propensities
which forms one of the principal characteristics of the
race in general.   An old woman, no light authority in
such matters, described them nearly in the words of the
author of the curious tract, " *Round about our Coal
Fire*," quoted in Brand, vol. ii. p. 279.
   Almost within the memory of persons still living it
was customary for the good woman of the cottage,
before she retired to rest, to carefully sweep the hearth,
and place thereon a vessel of water, to assist in the
ablutions, which it was believed formed a principal
object of their midnight visits ; and if perchance any of
the family woke during the night they heard the sound
of their tiny footsteps as they gambolled over the fast-
cooling hearth.   Unless espionage was attempted, pros-

perity always attended the household thus visited.
Tradition has recorded that a man whose house they so
frequented, and who had received many favours from
them, became smitten with a violent desire to behold
his invisible benefactors. Determined to indulge his
curiosity, and not having the fate of the Coventry worthy
before his eyes, he one night stationed himself behind
a knot in the door, which divided the " house" from the
sleeping apartment. True to their usual custom, the elves
came; but no sooner had he glanced at the objects of
his watch than he became blind : and so provoked were
the fairies at this breach of hospitality that they deserted his dwelling, and never more returned to it.*

The legends of all countries concur in describing milk
as the principal article of fairy diet. The Northamptonshire elves were noted for an inordinate love of it,
and did not scruple to obtain it by invading the privity
of the dairy ; nay, some impute to them the offence,
which is also alleged of the hedgehog, and declare that
they suck the cows as they sleep This is not the only
case in which they evince the laxity of their notions
respecting the human laws of *meum* and *teum*. Like
the Scottish good neighbours, and the Devonshire
pixies, they have little to recommend them on the score
of honesty. On the approach of midnight they leave
their " moonlight meadow rings" to feast upon the scanty
leavings of the cottage buttery ; taking care, however,
to lull the watchful eye of the housewife, by substituting
some unreal material for the edibles thus abstracted.
According to John Clare—

"Mice are not reckon'd greater thieves,
  They take away as well as eat,
  And still the housewife's eyes they cheat :
  In spite of all the folks that swarm,
  In cottage small, and larger farm,
  They through each keyhole pop and pop,
  Like wasps into a grocer's shop."

They are also represented as robbing those whom they dislike, in order to give the spoil to those who have gained their favour.

A worthy farmer, engaged in threshing, was sorely puzzled at the marvellous celerity with which his sheaves vanished : much faster, indeed, than accorded with the slow strokes of his flail. Extra bolts were placed on the doors, and a man stationed in the yard to watch ; still, however, the evil was unremedied, and each morning, though it found the fastenings untouched, brought with it a fresh gap in the mow. With the view of discovering the aggressors, Hodge determined upon a personal survey ; and late one night ensconced himself behind the sheaves for that purpose. Midnight soon came, and with it two tiny elves, who effected their entrance through the pike-hole, and forthwith commenced working away at the sheaves, pulling out the straws, and making them into minute bundles, preparatory to carrying them off. As may be readily imagined, this was little to Hodge's taste ; but though astonished and alarmed, he interfered not. At length, apparently overcome by their exertions, they desisted from their work. " I twit ; do you twit ? " said one to the other (*quasi*, I sweat ; do you sweat ?). " The devil twit ye ! " cried the farmer, rushing out, and totally unable any longer to conceal his indignation: "I'll twit ye if ye bent off!" At which the spirits instantly vanished, and never afterwards annoyed him with their visits.[b]

The gifts of the fairy-folk are, however, illusive and unreal. Among the numerous legends—

> "And thousands such the village keeps alive ;
> Beings that people superstitious earth ;
> That e'er in rural manners will survive,
> As long as wild rusticity has birth,"[*]

we have, in common with the Irish and Germans, the one in which the fairy money is represented as changing into paper. A more ludicrous instance is the following ; puerile, no doubt, but still valuable as a connecting link in the curious mythic chain:—A woodman went to the forest to fell some timber : just as he was applying the axe to the trunk of a huge old oak, out jumped a fairy, who beseeched him with the most supplicating gestures to spare the tree. Moved more by fright and astonishment than anything else, the man consented, and as a reward for his forbearance was promised the fulfilment of his three next wishes. Whether from natural forgetfulness, or fairy illusion, we know not, but certain it is, that long before evening all remembrance of his visitor had passed from his noddle. At night, when he and his dame were dozing before a blazing fire, the old fellow waxed hungry, and audibly wished for a link of hog's pudding. No sooner had the words escaped his lips than a rustling was heard in

* Clare's Village Minstrel, vol. I.

the chimney, and down came a bunch of the wished-for
delicacies, depositing themselves at the feet of the as-
tounded woodman, who, thus reminded of his morning
visitor, began to communicate the particulars to his wife.
" Thou bist a fool, Jan," said she, incensed at her husband's carelessness in neglecting to make the best of his
good luck ; " I wish em wer atte noäse!" whereupon,
the legend goes on to state, they immediately attached
themselves to the member in question, and stuck so
tight that the woodman, finding no amount of force
would remove these unsightly appendages from his
proboscis, was obliged, reluctantly, to wish them off :
thus making the third wish, and at once ending his
brilliant expectations.[c]

The affinity of our fairies with the whole kindred of
Teutonick *alfen* is still further developed by the great
partiality they evince for water.   In the shady stillness
of a summer's eve they took delight in bathing and
sporting among the waters of some lonely pond, or sedgy
bend of a rippling brook.   In some parts of the county
there are ponds which, from this circumstance, receive
the name of " fairy pools."   Near the village of Brington
is one so designated, where, I have been assured, a
few years ago they might be seen rollicking on the
surface, and gambolling among the water-plants which
lined the edges.   Wells are also favourite places of
their resort ; and there appears to be a vague species of
apprehension in the rustic mind at even passing a lonely
well after night-fall.   Shakespeare's elves, it will be
remembered, met—

" By paved fountain, or by rushy brook."

And Fletcher speaks of—

> " A virtuous well, about whose flowery banks
> The nimble-footed fairies dance their rounds."

The "green sour ringlets," frequently found on pasture land, are believed to be made by them ; and the fairy dwelling is supposed to exist under the area bordered by the dark circle. In the parish of Brington is one of these, which has attained such great local celebrity as to be called, *par excellence*, " *the* fairies' ring." It is believed to have existed from the earliest times, and to have resisted all the efforts of the plough to efface it, which, notwithstanding the awful calamities constantly attending such sacrilegious attempts, have, it is said, often been made. Village traditions relate that by running round it nine times on the first night of the full-moon sounds of mirth and revelry may be heard proceeding from the subterranean abode.

Like the Irish elves, who were adepts at ball-play, our fairies greatly delighted in all kinds of diversion. A South Northamptonshire legend tells of a young fellow who was fortunate enough to witness one of their sportive encounters. Returning home one moonlight night from a neighbouring village, where he had been partaking in the festive revelry of the feast-day, he fell in with a "vast o' fairy-folk," who, ·divided into two bodies, were fiercely contending at foot-ball. Undaunted at the strange scene, he joined their ranks, and mingled in the scuffle ; but no sooner did he succeed in striking the ball than it burst with a loud sound,—the elves vanished, and himself fell stunned to the ground. When he awoke his strange adventure appeared like a dream, but the scattered remains of the " bursten ball," thickly stuffed with golden coin, agreeably convinced him to the contrary.

THE BOGIE.

The Bogie was the household spirit ; the same with the Robin Goodfellow and Bogle of other parts of England. He played the same part among the old farm-houses and granges of Northamptonshire as the Brownies and Nisses did among the homesteads of Scotland and Sweden. His dwarfish stature, though somewhat larger than the ordinary race of elves, and his extreme love of mischief, show his connection with the other members of the same family. That he was a merry and jovial sprite we know from the proverb, " to laugh like old Bogie," or the old proverbial saying, " He caps Bogie," spoken of a person who is boisterously enjoying himself : often amplified to—

" He caps Bogie, Bogie capt Redcap, Redcap capt Nick."

Thus reducing the last-mentioned personage to the lowest point in the scale of conviviality. Our goblin does not appear to have been of so beneficent a character as the Highland Browny, who formed a valuable appendage to the household, and whose services were, at least, worth the " creame-bowl, duly set." His operations were, for the most part, confined to the grievously tormenting the family in whose abode he had taken up his residence. He it was whose nocturnal revels in some lonely garret, produced those never-to-be-explained sounds which chilled the hearts of superstitious servant-maids. But the cellar was the apartment in which he chiefly delighted ; there he reigned supreme, and, as old legends testify, imbibed the October at a terrible rate.

Among other characteristics of this spirit, was that of superior strength, a quality which he also holds in common with his German and Scandinavian brethren. It is to a being of this class that the village of Stowe, near Daventry, is said to derive its adjunct of " Nine-churches." In days of yore, say the villagers, a lord of the manor was desirous of raising a church in his native place, at that time known by the simple appellation of Stowe. A hill was chosen for the site, cunning workmen procured, and the foundation laid ; but on the following morning, when the labour was to be resumed, no traces of the yesterday's work were visible. Trenches, stones, and tools had all vanished. After a long search they were discovered, some distance beyond, on the spot where the present church now stands. The lord, however, was stubborn, and was not to be so easily baffled. Niné times did he renew his attempt, and each time were they frustrated by the spirit, who continued to remove in the night what the workmen had raised during the day. With great difficulty a man was induced to watch these midnight proceedings : and who does the reader imagine were the unseen opponents of the church builders ? The tiny legions of Queen Mab, perhaps, as in the case of God's Hill, in the Isle of Wight. But, alas! for the poetry of our rustics, the watchman reported the aggressor as an object "summet bigger nor a hog." After this the attempt was given up in despair, and the present church built on the site so marvellously selected.[d]

In spite of the advantages which his spirituality may be supposed to have afforded him, he appears to have wanted the superior cunning which characterize the more diminutive members of the elfin race. The following legend, very commonly narrated in Northamptonshire, places this in a strong light :—One of these spirits once asserted a claim to a field hitherto possessed by a farmer, and, after much disputing, they came to an arrangement by agreeing to divide its produce between them. At seed-time the farmer asks the Bogie what part of the crop he will have, "tops or bottoms." "Bottoms," said the spirit : upon hearing which his crafty antagonist sows the field with wheat, so that when harvest arrived the corn falls to his share, while the poor Bogie is obliged to content himself with the stubble. Next year the Bogie, finding he had made such an unfortunate selection in the bottoms, chose the "tops;" whereupon the crafty farmer sets the field with turnips—thus, again, outwitting the simple claimant. Tired of this unprofitable farming, the Bogie agrees to hazard his claims on a mowing match,—the land in question to be the stake for which they played. Before the day of meeting the canny earth-tiller procures a number of iron bars, which he strews among the grass to be mown by his opponent; and when the trial commences, the unsuspecting goblin finds his progress retarded by his scythe continually coming into contact with these obstacles, which he takes to be some hard species of dock. "Mortal hard docks these!" said he ; "Nation hard docks!" His blunted blade soon brings him to a stand-still ; and as, in such cases, it is not allowable for one to sharpen without the other, he turns to his antagonist, now far ahead, and in a tone of despair inquires—"When d'ye wiffle waffle (*whet*), mate ?" "Waffle!" said the farmer, with a well-feigned stare of amazement, " oh, about noon, mebby." "Then," said the despairing Bogie, " I've lost my land !" So saying, he disappeared, and the farmer reaped the reward of his artifice by ever afterwards continuing the undisputed possessor of the soil.ᵉ

With the exception of the proverbs and legends, few traces of him remain ; and time, which has cast a lenient eye upon his fellows, has been particularly hard upon the domestic spirit. His name, it is true, has yet terrors for unruly children ; but what a degradation for a goblin who was formerly the dread of full-grown ones ! The same waves among which tradition has assigned a resting place for the disorderly spirits of our ancestors, have also been the place of exile of the Bogies. "What has become of all these spirits ?" said we to a promising specimen of the *genus rusticus*, on whom we had been pursuing our researches. " What, arnt you heerd ?" was the response. " No," said we, with an ignorant look, expecting to elicit some inedited legend respecting their gradual extinction. " Why, then, I'll tell 'e : a deadly long time ago, the paasons all laid their yeads togither, *and hiked 'em off to the Red Saa !*"

THE REDMAN.

We have been able to collect but little concerning this member of our fairy family : he seems in all respects to have been similar to the elves, with the exception that while they were represented as living together in large communities, the Redman was an elf of solitary habits, residing in caves, old wells, &c. In some parts of the county he is called Redcap, from the colour of his head covering. In the southern districts he is called Redman, and described as a "small hairy dwarf." The only legend we have been able to recover represents him in a light very similar to the "Erdmanniken," of M. M. Grimm.'

HELL-HOUNDS, ETC.

The goblin huntsman and his train, the "wütend heer." of the German peasantry, are known to the good people of this county by the name of the "wild-men," "wild-hounds," &c. The Devonshire traditions represent the "yeth-hounds" as the disembodied souls of unbaptized infants ; but the Northamptonshire superstition is extremely vague and ill-defined. Both Whittlebury and Rockingham contend for the honour of his residence ; and the wild whoop with which he cheers his hounds is still said to be heard among the glades of both forests. According to a writer in the "Sporting Magazine," (1849, p. 60,) a Whittlebury tradition ascribes his origin to an incident similar to the one which forms the plot of the "Nastagio and Traversari," of Boccacio. A daughter of one of the noble rangers, famed at once for her beauty and coquetry, was an object of the deepest attachment to a gallant young knight; but his love and devotion, though at one time encouraged, was finally treated with coldness and contempt : driven to madness by her conduct, he put an end to his existence by plunging a sword into his heart. But, mark the retribution : the lady soon dies, and is doomed to be eternally hunted by the demon knight—

> " That she, whom I so long pursued in vain,
> Should suffer at my hands a lingering pain :
> Received to life that she may daily die ;
> I daily doomed to follow, she to fly."*

The forest of Whittlebury has been well stocked with deer since the days of the first king of England, and the midnight revels of goblin huntsmen may, in all probability, be traced to the deer-stealers, who, to avoid detection, would manifestly encourage a superstition furnishing such an admirable cloak for their depredations. The acephalous horseman is also well known in Northamptonshire ; and though our dialect is not rich enough to afford him a particular designation, we may boast possession of this veritable Dul hallan. He is confined to no particular district, but common to almost every parish in the county. On a calm summer's night, when the pale glimmer of the young moon scarcely penetrates the dark foliage of the trees, he may be seen mounted on his silent-hoofed steed, slowly riding along the green-sward border of some old green lane or lonely road, and woe to the benighted

* Dryden's version, " Theodore and Honoria."

traveller who crosses his path.   His appearance is
generally regarded as ominous of evil, often death.

In this class must also be placed the mischievous
goblin who prowls about the county in the guise of a
shaggy foal; sometimes deluding people into mounting
him, and then vanishing with a shout of fiendish
laughter.   " It's a common tradition in villages," says
John Clare, " that the devil often appears in the form
of a shagg'd foal; and a man in our parish firmly
believes that he saw him in that character one morning
early in harvest."*   The form of the foal, it will be
recollected, was one of Puck's favourite incarnations :—

> " Sometimes I meet them like a man,
>   Sometimes an ox, sometimes a hound,
> And to a horse I turn me can,
>   To trip and trot them round ;
>   But if to ride
>   My back they stride,
>   More swift than wind, away I go,
>   O'er hedge and lands,
>   Thro' pools and ponds,
>   I whirry, laughing ho, ho, ho !"

Compare with the *brag* of the Northern counties, the
colt-pixy of Hampshire, and the *grant* of Gervase (*Otia
imperialia*, D. iii. c. 52).

* Introduction to Village Minstrel, p. xxi.

WITCHCRAFT.

"How now, ye secret, black, and midnight hags,
    What is't you do?"

MACBETH.

THIS dark relic of paganism, fanned into flame by the
fanaticism of the Reformation, and only ceasing to be
recognised by the legislature, at the repeal of the witch
laws in 1738, still holds a conspicuous place among our
popular superstitions.

Reginald Scot defines witchcraft to be, "In the
estimation of the vulgar, a supernatural work, between
a corporall old woman and a spirituall devill." A
witch, then, according to the general acceptation, is an
old woman, who, by intercourse with the invisible
world, becomes possessed of supernatural influence,—
a power which she invariably exercises to her own
lucre, and the infinite discomfort of her neighbours.
Whatever may be the subtlety usually ascribed to her,
she cannot be accused of fighting under false colours.
She may be readily known by her sinister aspect, her
"wizzen'd" look, and her hairy lips.   She is unable to
assuage her grief by weeping; and must, moreover, evince
a decided partiality for black cats.   Moroseness is also
another of her qualities: to this day the phrase, "as
cross as a witch," conveys the idea of exceeding irasci-

L

bility. Besides this species, which, for distinction's sake, we may denominate the witch proper, there is supposed to exist another variety, totally distinct from the former, inasmuch as their ranks are not recruited from the old and ill-favoured—are not confined to the female sex—and are undiscoverable by any of the outward peculiarities which mark the elder sisterhood. These beings, like the witches of Cervantes, appear to do nothing that leads to any object.   They spend their nights, for the most part, in the delectable occupation of riding over the woods and wastes, showing in this, and other characteristics, a strong affinity with " *les brous*" of the peasantry of Tourraine. These must, on no account, be confounded with the " white witches" of old writers, who took their rise when witch-finding had become a profitable profession.   Their place in Northamptonshire was occupied by the " cunning man ;" who, by a certain " demonaicall complaisance," as Master Bovet calls it, was permitted to apply his art to the counteraction of their spells.

The ideas of our peasantry concerning witchcraft differ, in many respects, from the strange medley of native superstition and exotic fiction preserved under that name in the writings of the demonologists.   In the Northamptonshire legends we find but slight traces of the imp-familiars, and other diabolical phenomena, which shed so horrible a glow over the relations of Scot and Hopkins.   In this peculiarity we imagine we discern traces of an earlier and less repulsive belief; in which, as in the early Scotch trials, the place of the tempter was occupied by the " kingdom of faerie."   The solemn compacts with Satan, so graphically described by Gaule, are also wanting in the Northamptonshire traditions. Our initiatory ceremony was very simple. The person desirous of becoming a witch was to sit on *the hob of the hearth ;* and, after carefully cleaning and paring her nails, to give utterance to the words—" I wish I was as far from God as my nails are from dirt :" whereupon the experimenter immediately becomes possessed of powers which place at her mercy all those who have had the misfortune to incur her displeasure. Her operations are, however, under some restraint : she cannot exercise any influence over those who firmly refuse to give her anything ; but if the request be complied with, or the refusal be accompanied with any qualifying phrase, she is at full liberty to pursue her schemes on the donor—a belief which, ridiculous as it may seem, has often prevented the exercise of charity.

Tradition has also preserved another article of the belief, which will be of some assistance in a scientific investigation of this fearful monomania. Witchcraft, like hydrophobia, was contagious. The person bit or scratched by a witch immediately became one.

Rapidly as such an absurd chimera is being rooted out by the progress of education, the legends concerning it do not bid fair to be so soon erased from the tablet of tradition. Even were it desirable, it would be an hopeless task to collect one tithe of the tales still told by the " gammer" to a shuddering audience round the cottage fire.

" She from her memory oft repeats,
   Witches dread powers, and fairy feats :

How one has oft been known to prance,
In cow-crib, like a coach, to France ;
And ride on sheep-trays from the fold,
A race-horse speed, to Barton-hold,
To join the midnight mystery's rout,
Where witches meet the yews about."*

Among the most common of these stories, are those in which the witch is represented as metamorphosing herself into some animal, and while in that state receiving some personal injury, appears maimed when she resumes her human shape, by which means her infernal connection is discovered.†

A cat is the animal most commonly favoured with these transformations. A woodman out working in the forest has his dinner every day stolen by a cat : exasperated at the continued repetition of the theft, he lies in wait for the aggressor, and succeeds in cutting off her paw ; when, lo! on his return home he finds his wife minus a hand. Sometimes a fox or hare : old huntsmen still tell of the witch of Wilby, and the famous "chivvies" she used to lead the hounds. Nor are these curious transformations confined to the animal kingdom : a tree is not unfrequently selected. A few years ago, one to which a legend of this kind was attached, was standing in the village of Syresham. The tradi-

* Clare's " Shepherd's Calendar," p. 10.

† A similar trait occurs in the confessions of the Scotch witches :
" The dowgis will som tymes get som bytis of us quhan we ar in hairis, bot will not get us killed. Quhan we turn out of a hairis liknes to our awin shap, we will haw the bitis, scrattis, &c., in our bodies."
—*Conf. of Isabell Gowdie. Pitcairn's Scotch Criminal Trials,* vol. iii. p. 610.

tion concerning it relates that a man was one day passing
by it, when a little boy, who accompanied him, begged
for a branch to play with.   The man consented, drew
his knife, and began to cut, when, *horribile dictu !* a
stream of blood instantly spouted from the incision he
had made.   A woman of the village, long suspected to
be " not quite right," soon after made her appearance
with one of her arms bound up ; and, if we recollect
right, the pseudo tree finished her career in a neighbouring pond, where she was subjected to the water
ordeal.   It would be foreign to our purpose to descant
upon the often-told history of the old lady, whose feats
in the bewitching line reached such a pitch of presump-
tion that she became turned into stone ; and still remains (where, my informant saith not) a striking
monument of the Almighty vengeance : but we cannot
resist pointing out the connexion which obviously exists
between witchcraft and the elf-lore of popular superstition.   No exploit attributed to the witch but finds its
parallel among the feats of the faëry ; and the affinity
is still further illustrated by a comparison of the stories,
many of which closely assimilate to the fairy legends of
other districts.   Thus, for instance, we have a tale
nearly resembling the Irish legend, " Master and Man,"
in which the place of the elf is occupied by a wizzard
and his wife.   In the Irish legend, a man becomes the
servant of a Cluricaune, and assists his master in an
attempt to abduct a young lady about to become the
bride of another.   While lying in wait for their prey,
the bride sneezes, and Pat, unable to resist the force of
habit, twice returns the customary blessing, which

causes the failure of the enterprise. In the Northamptonshire version, a young fellow "lets hissel" to a
farmer and his wife, who, from their nightly journey-
ings on calves, he quickly discovers to be no less personages than witches. One night he is required to
attend them on one of these unhallowed expeditions,
the object of which is the stealing of a child, to be used,
probably, in the midnight orgies round the cauldron.
Previous to their starting he is enjoined to refrain from
giving utterance to the sacred name,—a word fraught with
terror to goblins of all denominations, from the demons of
the "Legenda aurea," who vanish at the solemn " In
nomine Patris" of the cowl, to the Arabian fiend of
Scheherazade, who dropped his rider at the mention of
Allah. Twice on the road did the awkwardness of his
steed call forth imprecations, in which were mingled
the name of the forbidden one ; and while preparing to
pass through the last keyhole which divided them from
the infant, so beset was he with the fear of remaining
stationary therein, that, forgetting his orders, in an
agony of terror, he ejaculated, " God save us !" an exclamation which, as my narrator proceeded to inform
me, " geunne *he* the sack, but saved the babby."

Besides the somewhat doubtful power of the cunning
man, certain charms and amulets were (and still are)
resorted to in order to procure immunity from the arts
of the witch. Among the most common of these was
the " lucky bone." (*See* p. 154.) A stone, with a hole
through it, was also highly esteemed. Morton, in his
Natural History of Northamptonshire, speaking of perforated pebbles, remarks : " Those that are perforated

with only a single hole of large bore the vulgar here are
wont to use as amulets, hanging them up in stables,
and at their beds-heads, imagining they have a strange
and wonderful efficacy against the powers of witchcraft."* The horseshoe was another preventive. One
that has been found, nailed above the threshold, or
suspended over the hearth, is supposed to be highly efficacious. Houses so protected, though unquestionably
less than formerly, are still by no means few. Crossed
straws† and knives laid on the cottage floor are also held
in high repute. A credulous old dame informed the
compiler that she once tested this *experimentum crucis:*
having long entertained shrewd suspicions as to the
"rightness" of one of her neighbours, she invited her to
her cottage; but previous to her coming placed the knives
in an obscure corner. The suspected arrived, but would
on no account sit down, and soon after retired in evident confusion; thus at once confirming the superstition of the good woman, and increasing her faith in the
efficacy of her charm.

Northamptonshire appears to have been early connected with witchcraft. In the reign of Edward IV.
we find "oon John Daunger, parishe clerk of Stoke
Brewerne," accused of having in his possession an
"ymage of led," made by the Duchess of Gloucester,
who was charged with having, by means of it, fixed

* This charm is also found in Scot's " Discovery of Witchcraft,"
1584.

† So in Addison's character of the witch, in his Sir Roger de
Coverley papers :—" If she chanced to stumble they always found
sticks or *straws* that lay in the form of a *cross* before her."

the love of the king on her daughter Elizabeth.[*]   In
1612, the execution of some witches gave rise to that
scarce black-letter, "The Witches of Northamptonshire;" and brochures of a similar character were published to celebrate the execution of another batch in
1705, and the last execution for witchcraft at Northampton, July 22nd, 1712.   The 22nd relation of
Glanville's "*Saducismus Triumphatus*" is occupied by
a curious case which occurred at Welton, near Daventry,
in 1658, in which, among other equally strange phenomena, a young girl, ten years of age, is said to have
"vomited, in less than three days, three gallons of
water, to their great admiration.   After this," continues
the credulous narrator, "the elder wench comes running
and tells them that now her sister begins to vomit
stones and coals.   They went, and were eye-witnesses :
told them till they came to five hundred.   Some
weighed a quarter of a pound, and were so big as they
had enough to do to get them out of her mouth,"
&c. &c.

The swimming ordeal was formerly practised in this
county.   Hutchinson, in his *Historical Essay on Witchcraft*, under the date 1692, observes, " Several witches
were tried by swimming in Northamptonshire, &c. ;"
"and," adds he, "some drownd in the tryal."   The
last authenticated instance that we have been able to
discover occurred in 1785, and is thus referred to in a
Northampton Mercury of that year : " A poor woman,

---

[*] Extracts from Rolls of Parliament, 9th Edward IV., given in
Wright's Proceedings against Dame Kyteler.

named Sarah Bradshaw, of Mears Ashby, who was accused by some of her neighbours of being a witch, in order to prove her innocence, submitted to the ignominy of being dipped, when she immediately sunk to the bottom of the pond, which was deemed to be an incontestable proof that she was no witch."

CHARMING.

There are few villages in Northamptonshire, the Southern district especially, which are not able to boast a professor of the healing art, in the person of an old woman, who pretends to the power of curing diseases by charming; and at the present day, in spite of coroner's inquests and parish officers, the belief in the efficacy of these remedies appears to be undiminished. Two preliminaries are given as necessary to be observed in order to ensure a perfect cure. First, that the person to be operated upon comes with an earnest belief that a cure *will* be effected; and secondly, that the phrases " please" and " thank you" do not occur during the transaction. The established formula consists in the charmer's crossing the part affected, and whispering over it certain mysterious words—doubtless varied according to the disorder, but the import of which it is difficult to discover, there being a very prevalent notion that if once disclosed they would lose their virtue. In some cases it is customary for the charmer to " bless" or hallow cords or leathern-thongs, which are given to the invalid to be worn round the neck. An old woman, living at a village near Brackley, has acquired more than ordinary renown for the cure of agues by this

means. According to her own account, she received
the secret from the dying lips of her mother; who, in
her turn, is said to have received it from hers.   As the
old dame is upwards of ninety, and still refuses to part
with her charm, the probability of its perishing with
her forms a constant theme of lamentation among her
gossips.   It must not be supposed that these ignorant
people make a trade of their supposed art : on the contrary, it is believed that any offer of pecuniary remune-
ration would break the spell, and render the charm of
no avail.   Though it must be admitted that the influence and position' naturally accruing to the possessor
of such attributes affords a sufficient motive for imposture, we think, for the most part, that they may be
said to be the dupes of their own credulity, and as fully
convinced of their own powers as can be the most credulous of their admirers.   A collection of traditionary
charms current among the rural population of this
county will be found in *Notes and Queries*, vol. ii. pp.
36, 37.

The *lucky-bone*, as its name indicates, is worn about
the person to produce good-luck; and is also reckoned
an excellent protection against witchcraft.   It is a bone
taken from the head of a sheep, and its form, which is
that of the T cross, may have, perhaps, originated the
peculiar sanctity in which it is held.   This form of the
sacred symbol is frequently found on Druidical monu-
ments.   Vide *Report of the Royal Cornwall Institution*,
1846; *Ecclesiologist*, No. 28, February 1848.

West.—In order to be rid of the painful tumor on
the eyelid, provincially known as the *west*, or sty, it is

customary for the sufferer, on the first night of the new
moon, to procure the tail of a black cat, and after
pulling from it one hair, rub the tip nine times over the
pustule.   As this has a very cabalistic look, and is,
moreover, frequently attended with sundry severe
scratches, a gold ring is found to be a much more harmless substitute, and is now more commonly used.   This
superstition is alluded to by Beaumont and Fletcher,
Mad Lovers, v. 4.

> "—— I have a sty here, Chilax.
>   CHI. I have no gold to cure it, not a penny."

Thorn.—The following word-charm is used to prevent a thorn from festering :—

> " Our Saviour was of a virgin born,
>   His head was crowned with a crown of thorn ;
>   It never canker'd nor fester'd at all ;
>   And I hope in Christ Jesus this never shaull (shall).

This will remind the reader of the one given by Pepys,
vol. ii. p. 415.

SUPERSTITIONS RELATING TO ANIMALS.*

Mice.—A sudden influx of mice into a house hitherto
free from their ravages, denotes approaching mortality
among its inhabitants.   A mouse running over a person
is considered to be an infallible sign of death ; as is also

---

* Reprinted, with additions, from Notes and Queries, vol. ii. p.
37, and 164-5.

the squeaking of one behind the bed of an invalid, or the apparition of a white mouse running across the room. To meet with a shrew-mouse in going a journey is reckoned ominous of evil. The country people have an idea that the harvest-mouse is unable to cross a path which has been trod by man. Whenever they attempt, they are immediately, as my informant expressed it, "struck dead." This, they say, accounts for the numbers which, on a summer's evening, may be found lying dead on the verge of the field foot-paths, without any external wound or apparent cause for their demise.

Poultry.—The crowing of a hen bodes evil; and is frequently followed by the death of some member of the family. When, therefore, Dame Partlet thus experiments upon the voice of her mate, she pays her head as the price of her temerity, a complete severance of the offending member being supposed to be the only way of averting the threatened calamity. No house, it is said, can thrive whose hens are addicted to this kind of amusement. Hence the old proverb, often quoted in Northamptonshire—

> " A whistling woman, and a crowing hen,
> Is neither fit for God nor men."

According to Pluquet, the Normans have a similar belief, and a saying singularly like the English one—

> " Une poule qui chante le coq, et une fille qui siffle, portent malheur dans la maison."

Before the death of a farmer his poultry frequently go to roost at noon-day, instead of at the usual time. When the cock struts up to the door, and sounds his clarion on the threshold, the housewife is warned that she may soon expect a stranger. In what is technically termed " setting a hen," care is taken that the nest be composed of an odd number of eggs. If even, the chickens would not prosper : each egg is marked with a small black cross, ostensibly for the purpose of distinguishing them from the others, but also supposed to be instrumental in preserving them from the attack of the weasel and other farm-yard marauders. The last egg the hen lays is carefully preserved, its possession being supposed to operate as a charm upon the well-doing of the poultry. In some cases, though less frequently, the one laid on Good Friday was kept for the same reason. When an infant is first taken out to see its friends, it is customary for them to give it an egg ; this, if preserved, is held to be a source of good fortune to the future man. (Vide *Brand*, ii. p. 48.)

Toads.—For stopping or preventing bleeding at the nose, a toad is killed by transfixing it with some sharp-pointed instrument ; after which it is enclosed in a little bag, and suspended round the neck. The same charm is also occasionally used in cases of fever. The following passage from Sir K. Digby's *Discourse on Sympathy* (Lond. 1658), may enlighten us as to the principle :—

" In time of common contagion, they use to carry about them the powder of a toad, and sometimes a living toad or spider, shut up in a box ; or else they carry arsenick, or some other venomous substance, which draws into it the contagious air, which otherwise would infect the party." p. 77.

Snakes.—There is a very prevalent belief that a snake can never die till the sun is down. Cut or hack it as you will it will never die till sunset. This idea has evidently its source in the amazing vitality common to the species.

Hares.—The running of a hare along the main street of a village forebodes a fire in the immediate vicinity. The right fore-foot of a hare worn constantly in the pocket is considered a fine amulet against the " rheumatiz." Scot, in his *Discovery of Witchcraft*, places under the head of " Wonderful Natural Effects," the bone of a hare's foot, which he says " mitigateth the cramp."

Robins and Wrens.—The robin is considered a sacred bird : to kill one is little less than sacrilege, and its eggs are free from the destroying hand of the bird-nester. It is asserted that the respect shown to it by man is also joined in by the animals of the wood. The weasel and wild cat, it is said, will neither molest it, nor eat it when killed. The high favour in which this bird is held is usually attributed to the ballad of *The Babes in the Wood.* Few, however, of our peasantry have ever heard of it ; and however much that beautiful tale may have tended to popularise the belief, it is evident that we must trace the origin to a more remote source. One cause for the veneration in which it is held may be the superstition which represents him as the medium through which mankind are warned of approaching death. Before the death of a person, a robin is believed, in many instances, to tap thrice at the window of the room in which he or she may be. The wren is also a bird which superstition preserves from wanton injury ; but is by no means treated with such reverence as the robin. The praises of both are sung in the old couplet—

> " The robin and the wren
> Be God A'mighty's cock and hen."

Cuckoos.—When the cry of the cuckoo is heard for the first time in the season, it is customary to turn the money in the pocket and wish. If within the bounds of reason, it is sure to be fulfilled.

Owls.—The ominous screech of this, the most ominous of all birds, is still heard with alarm ; and he remains with us, as in Chaucer's days—

> " The oule eke that of death the bode bringeth."

When, as sometimes happens, he exchanges the darkness of his ivy-bush for the rays of the sun at noon-day, his presence is looked upon as indicative of bad luck to the beholder.

Bees.—The superstitious ceremonies and observances attached to those insects appear to be current throughout the kingdom, and by no means suffer any diminution in Northamptonshire : among others of less common occurrence, we have the belief that they will not thrive in a quarrelsome family.

The wild, or, as we term him, the *bumble* bee, is not without a share of the superstitions which pertain to his more civilized brethren. The entrance of one into a cottage is deemed a certain sign of death.

Wasps.—The first wasp seen in the season should always be killed; by so doing you secure to yourself good luck and freedom from enemies throughout the year.

Spiders.—The small spiders, called "money-spinners," bring good luck to those on whom they alight; in order to propitiate which, they must be whirled over the shoulder. This belief is alluded to by Fuller (*Worthies*, p. 58, pt. ii.)—"When a spider is found upon our clothes, we use to say, some money is coming towards us;" which he moralizes after his quaint fashion—"Such who imitate the industry of that contemptible creature may, by God's blessing, weave themselves into wealth, and procure a plentiful estate."

Hedgehogs.—Among other animals looked upon in a superstitious light we have the hedgehog, who, in addition to his still credited attribute of sucking cows as they sleep, is looked upon by our rustics as the very emblem of craft and cunning; holding the same place in our popular stories as Reynard in the more Southern *fabliaux*, and of whom they relate the myth given by MM. Grimm concerning the race between the hare and the hedgehog. The Northamptonshire version makes the trial of speed between a fox and hedgehog; in all other respects our tale is word for word with the German.

Pigeons.—No one, it is believed, can die on pigeons' feathers. In the Northern parts of the county the same thing is said of game feathers: a superstition also current in Kent. *Ingoldsby Legends*, third series, p. 133.

Crows.—To see a crow flying alone is a token of

bad luck. An odd one perched in the path of the observer is a sign of wrath : thus Clare—

> " Odd crows settled on the path,
>   Dames from milking trotting home,
> Said the sign forboded wrath,
>   And shook their heads at ills to come."

Omens of misfortune or bad luck are also drawn from the " squining" of swine, the flying of swallows or jackdaws down the chimney, the chattering of magpies, and the desertion of an hearth by crickets. The two first are alluded to in, *Gaule's Mago-Astronomancers Pozed and Puzzled*, p. 181.

PLANT-SUPERSTITIONS.

Dane's-weed.—" From Daventry we went a little out of the road to see a great camp, called Burrow Hill, upon the north end of an eminence, cover'd over with fern and goss. . . . . . They say this was a Danish camp, and everything hereabouts is attributed to the Danes, because of the neighbouring Daventry, which they suppose to be built by them. The road hereabouts, too, being overgrown with Dane-weed, they fancy it sprang from the blood of the Danes slain in battle ; and that if, upon a certain day in the year, you cut it, it bleeds."—*De Foe's Tour of a Gentleman*, vol. ii. p. 362.

Apple-trees.—If an apple-tree bear at the same time

M

both blossom and fruit, it bodes death to some of the owner's family.

Flowers in coffins.—The custom of placing in the coffin, with the corpse, the most beautiful flowers that can be procured is still retained in the Southern district.   At the burial of an elderly person they are mingled with small sprigs of box and yew. Sir Thomas Overbury alludes to a similar custom : describing the character of " a faire and happy milk-maid," he finishes with—" Thus lived she ; and all her care is that she may die in the spring time, to have store of flowers stucke upon her winding-sheet."—*Characters*, 1615.

Plant-divinations.—Children pick the leaves of the herb called " pick-folly," one by one, repeating each time the words—" Rich man, poor man, beggar man, thief," &c., fancying that the one which comes to be named at the last plucking will prove the condition of their future partners.   Young maidens also place in their bosoms the empty head of the knot-weed, supposing that if they guess aright the swain—

> " Their loves' sweet fancies try to gain,"

it will blossom a second time ere it has remained an hour.   Another divination is likewise practised with blades of grass ; thus described by Clare :—

> " We laid two blades across, and lapt them round,
>   Thinking of those we loved ; and if we found
>   Them linked together when unlapt again,
>   Our loves were true : if not, the wish was vain.
>   I've heard old women, who first told it me,
>   Vow that a truer token could not be."

To find them unlapt three times in succession is held
to be very unlucky. To find an even ash is reckoned
very lucky, as is also the finding of nine peas in a
" kid."

Nuts.—The discovery of a double nut presages well
for the finder ; and unless he mars his good fortune by
swallowing both kernels, is considered an infallible sign
of approaching " luck." The orthodox way in such
cases consists in eating one, and throwing the other over
the shoulder. A double nut is often worn in the pocket
as a charm against toothache.

Ivy.—In decorating the house with evergreens at
Christmas, care must be taken not to let ivy be used
alone, or even predominate, as it is a plant of bad
omen, and will prove injurious.

WELLS AND SPRINGS.

THE custom of dedicating wells and springs remarkable
for their curative properties to particular saints, appears
to have obtained to some extent in this county.

Among the principal we may mention the celebrated
one of St. Laurence, at Peterborough, the superstitious
resort to which was the subject of an inhibition from the
Bishop of Lincoln, about the end of the twelfth century
(*Gunton's History of Peterboro'*, p. 227) ; the one dedicated to St. John, at Boughton, to which we must
look, in all probability, for the origin of the celebrated
fair annually held there ; St. Rumbald's well, at

Brackley, where, as Leland informs us, " they say that
within a fewe dayes of his birth he preched ;" the well
of St. Loy, or Eligius, at Weedon-Loys, of which
Morton says—" I take to be the chief of all the
Western part of the county.   Even blind and leprous
people, as tradition tells us, it infallibly cured ;" and
the notable spring of St. Dennis, at Naseby, to which it
was customary to bring children who had a weakness
in their limbs, and dip them in it *nine* mornings successively.   Wells dedicated to Saints Mary, Thomas
à Becket, Vincent, Helen, &c., exist also at Hardwick,
Northampton, Cosgrave, and Oxenden.   " The same
holy reverence," observes Morton,* " appears to have
been given to divers other fountains with us, and particularly those that still retain the name of Holy wells,"
a designation applied, in his time, to more than a dozen
mineral springs in different parts of the county.   Many
of these still retain their title, and their waters are still
considered efficacious for external application.   Such
names as Rood-well, Cross-well, Monk's-well, are of
frequent occurrence.   We must not omit to include in
our category the celebrated Drumming-well, at Oundle,
which, before any important national event, gave forth
sounds like the roll of a drum.   " When I was a school-
boy at Oundle, in Northamptonshire," says Baxter, in
his *World of Spirits*, p. 157, " about the Scots coming
into England, I heard a well, in one Dob's yard, beating
like any drum beating a march.   I heard it at a distance ; then I went and put my head into the mouth

---

* Natural History of Northampton, p. 283.

of the well, and heard it distinctly, and nobody in the well. It lasted several days and nights, so as all the country people came to hear it. And so it drumm'd on several changes of the times. When King Charles the Second died I went to the Oundle carrier, at the Ram Inn, in Smithfield, who told me their well had drummed, and many people came to hear it. And I heard it drummed once since."

Another presaging spring is described by Morton, "called Marvel-sike Spring, in Boughton Field, about two bows' shoot from Brampton Bridge, nigh Kingsthorp Road. It never runs but in mighty gluts of wet, and whenever it does is thought ominous by the country people, who, from the breaking out of that spring, are wont to prognosticate dearth, the death of some great personage, or very troublesome times. It did not run when I was there, on October 22nd, 1703, but the foregoing winter it did, and had not run before for two years. That winter it is well known was a very wet one, and observable for the breaking out of such springs as these." Dr. Plot, in his *Natural History of Staffordshire*, describes many similar springs in that county. Traces also yet linger of a darker and more ancient superstition connected with wells and fountains—that which represents their immediate vicinity as the favourite resort of the elves, and their dark waters the abode of the well-sprite. In the village of Aynho is a spring called *Puck-well*, which, we think, may be allowably referred to—

> "——— that shrewd and knavish sprite
> Call'd Robin Goodfellow."

MISCELLANEOUS SUPERSTITIONS.

SYMPATHY.

THE principle of sympathetic influence enters largely into the composition of our charms and popular remedies. To cure a wart, rub it with a piece of meat, which must be afterwards buried ; and as fast as the flesh rots the wart will decay. Another for the same :—Take one of the large black snails which are to be found, during the summer, in every hedgerow, rub it over the wart, and then hang it on a thorn. This must be done nine nights successively, at the end of which time the wart will completely disappear. For, as the snail exposed to such cruel treatment will gradually wither away, so it is believed the wart, being impregnated with its matter, will slowly do the same. The cure of wens by the " dead-stroke," is also another instance of the same idea (Vide *Brand*, vol. iii. p. 153).

If a horse gets a nail in his foot, it must be kept bright after it is taken out, or the horse will not recover from his lameness. Also current in Norfolk. *Forby's East Anglian Vocabulary*, vol. ii. p. 414.

When you cut your hair always be careful to burn it : if you throw it away, ten to one but some bird seizes it to assist in making its nest, and then you would be afflicted with a terrible headache. Teeth, also, when pulled out, must be covered with salt, and thrown into the fire. The curious article of the popular

faith which thus ascribes to salt the power of counter-
acting the injurious tendencies of sympathetic influence
is alluded to in Sir Kenelm Digby's *Discourse on Sympathy* (Lond. 1658). Boasting to the Frenchmen of
the riches and fertility of England, he observes :—

"There's not the meanest cottager but hath a cow to fur-
nish his family with milk. It is the principal sustenance of
the poorer sort of people, as 'tis also in Switzerland, which
makes them very carefull in the good-keeping and health of
their cowes. Now, if it happen that in boyling the milk it
swells so high that it shed over the brim of the skillet, and so
comes to fall into the fire, the goodwoman or maid does pre-
sently give over whatsoever she is doing, and runs to the
skillet, which she takes off the fire, and at the same time takes
a *handfull of salt*, which useth to be commonly in the corner
of the chimney to keep it dry, and throws it upon the cinders
whereon the milk was shed. Ask her wherefore she doth
so, and she will tell you that it is to prevent the cow which
gave the milk may not have some hurt upon her udder; for
without this remedy it would come to be hard and ulcerated,
and so be in order to die."

CROSSING.

Notwithstanding the long series of years which have
elapsed since the Reformation, numerous traces of
Romanism may still be found in our rural districts.
Protestant children still preface their slumbers with an
invocation to the apostles :—

"Matthew, Mark, Luke, and John,
Bless the bed that I lay on :
There be four corners to my bed,
I hope there be four angels spread :
One to watch, and two to pray,
And one to carry my soul away."

Sometimes, also, accompanied with an address to the Virgin, commencing in true alliterative style—

"Mary, mother, meek and mild."

The popular belief in ghosts, too, distinctly recognises the existence of a middle state, to which the soul of the good man goes, while that of the evil doer rests in its "wormy bed" till the day of resurrection; and the belief in the curative powers of the form of the cross still holds its sway in the popular mind. We retain such a high sense of its efficacy, that in case of spasms, or that painful state of the feet in which they are said to "sleep," it is commonly used, under the impression that it mitigates, if not entirely allays, the pain. Warts are also charmed away by crossing them with elder sticks; and a very common charm for the cramp consists in the sufferer's always taking care when he pulls off his shoes and stockings to place them in such a position as to form a resemblance to the "holy sign."

Crossing the dough is commonly practised, and is believed to make the bread come quicker. Herrick alludes to this in the *Hesperides* :—

> "This I'll tell ye by the way,
> Maidens, when ye leavens lay,
> Cross your dow, and your dispatch
> Will be better for your batch."

If a person wash in the water which another person has washed in, he and that person will quarrel before the day is out, unless the latter, before commencing his ablutions, takes the precaution of making the form of the cross with his finger on the water. Some, however, contend that the safest course is to use the old pagan charm of the saliva, and spit into the bowl; and some do both. Puissant, indeed, must be the *diablerie* to resist such potent disenchanters.

DAYS LUCKY AND UNLUCKY.

Friday is a very unlucky day. It is very dangerous even to turn the bed: on Friday, therefore, the good housewife allows the bed to remain unturned. Concerning it we have the proverbs, " Friday is either the fairest or foulest day of the week ;" and—

> "Such as Friday,
> So is Sunday."

Alluding, probably, to the connection between them in the history of the Resurrection. Monday and Thursday are the most propitious days for marriage.

The sun shines, if only for a minute, on every Saturday throughout the year. The Spaniards had a similar saying. See Southey's *Doctor*, vol. iii. p. 165.

Saturday and Sunday are unlucky days for servants to go to their places : thus the saying—

> " Saturday servants never stay,
> Sunday servants run away."

FINDING.

To find a horse-shoe is lucky ; but to find a knife, just the reverse. To find iron also presages good fortune ; but to find silver, however acceptable it may be at the time, is sure to prove unlucky to the finder.

" Whereas it is ordinarie to diuine of future things by some such like, as by finding a piece of iron, signifying good lucke,—

but if siluer be found then it is euill,—to haue a hare crosse the way,—to haue the salt fall towards him, &c.,—these, hauing no such uirtue from heauen and diuine ordination, it must needs follow that they are diabolical, or at least superstitious, and no way warrantable."—*Cooper's Mystery of Witchcraft,* 1617, p. 137.

MOON, STARS, ETC.

Never point at the moon or stars, it is very unlucky. It is, also, considered to be highly unlucky to first see the new moon through glass : to see it aright, it should be gazed on from over the left shoulder, and the beholder should wish.   As an instance of the adaptation of popular stories and traditions to suit the peculiarities of different localities, we may mention that the Northamptonshire version of the myth which accounts for the existence of that mysterious personage ycleped the Man-in-the-moon, represents him as condemned to his solitary life through his having stolen a *furze* faggot on a Sunday.   According, however, to the ideas of our rustics, it is the Sabbath-breaking which constituted the principal offence, and not, as Chaucer represents, the theft :—

> " On his brest a chorle painted ful even,
>   Bearing a bush of thorns on his backe,
>   Which, for his theft, might clime no ner the heven."[*]

DEATH TOKENS.

Of all omens, none are more numerous, or so implicitly credited, as those which are supposed to presage death.   Almost every incident out of the common

---

[*] Testament of Creseid, v. 38.

course of natural events, or which cannot be explained by the ordinary principles of rustic philosophy, is looked upon as ominous of approaching mortality. Among the most common of these not included in any of the preceding divisions, are the flowering of a tree twice in one year, or the sudden dropping of an article of furniture without any apparent cause; and even the household clock has been known to depart from its customary precision in order to warn its owner by striking *thirteen!* Others, again, are of a more direct spiritual agency, such as three knocks upon the wall of the sick man's apartment—the sudden call of a person's name, proceeding, as it were, from the air—or the heavy sound of the death-coach, which, though now never *seen*, is still *heard* rumbling along the old lanes.

DIVINATIONS.

Divination by the *Sortes sanctorum* is still common in this county.   On New Year's day the master of the family opens the Bible with his eyes shut, and the passage first touched by his finger is interpreted to refer to the events of the coming year.

A divination is also practised with respect to the weather, by narrowly observing the atmospheric changes of the first twelve days of the new year : each day standing for a month, and forming an index to the weather of the period of which it is the numerical representative.

Hairy persons always go to heaven.

A child who has a sufficient space between the middle

teeth of his front row to pass a small coin through, is born to be lucky.

When two persons in conversation are going to tell each other the same thing, it is a sign that some lie will soon be told about them.

The shilling given to servants as "earnest" money must be spent immediately, or they will neither stay long nor be fortunate at the place they are going to.

Mirrors are favourite objects of superstition: the breakage of one portends death or bad luck, limited, according to some, for seven years. It is also considered highly injurious to let a child look in one before it is a year old.

Smoke and dust always follow the fairest. One of the errors refuted by Sir Thomas Browne.

A pair of knives crossed, or the noise made by the steam in escaping from a block of wood while burning, presage a quarrel.

A person who often has his hair in his mouth will become a drunkard.

Birds' eggs should never be kept in the house, they are very unlucky. A superstition to be found in *Hone's Year Book*, p. 253.

In the pocket of a rustic will be frequently found a small piece of dried flesh : this, he will tell you, is the tip of a calf's tongue, and is called a "*lucky bit.*" He considers it to be wonderfully efficacious in all cases of assault and battery, ensuring to its possessor the privilege of coming out unscathed. It is also possessed of the valuable property of producing a constant supply of ready cash, inasmuch as there is a saying that the pocket which contains it will never be without money.

Servants who go to their places in black will never stay the year out.

NICK.

It now only remains to notice the third person of the curious mythological trinity preserved in the proverb at page 138. " The legendary Satan," says a writer in the *Quarterly Review* (vol. xxii. p. 353), "is a being wholly distinct from the theological Lucifer. He is never ennobled by the sullen dignity of the fallen angel. No traces of celestial origin are to be discerned on his brow. He is not a rebellious *Æon*, who once was clothed in radiance. But he is the fiend, the enemy : evil from all time past; in his very essence foul and degraded, cowardly and impure : his rage is oftenest impotent, unless his cunning can assist his power. He excites fright rather than fear. Hence wild caprice and ludicrous malice are his popular characteristics ; they render him familiar, and diminish the awe inspired by his name ; and these playful elements enter into all the ghost and goblin combinations of the evil principle." As depicted in the Northamptonshire legends, he still continues the horned, fanged, and tailed goblin who frayed our ancestors of good Reginald Scot's days,* a

* "In our childhood our mothers' maids have so terrified us with an ugly devil, having horns on his head, fire in his mouth, and a tail in his breech, eyes like a bason, fangs like a dog, claws like a bear, a skin like a niger, and a voyce roaring like a lyon, whereby we start and are afraid when we hear one cry *Bough !*"—*Discovery of Witchcraft*, p. 85.

worthy representative of the fiend who figures so largely in those pious romances, the *Lives of the Saints ;*—the tempter of St. Anthony, and the tormentor of the holy hermits, Godric and Guthlac, in their solitary residences among the wastes and fens. His intercourse with mankind has suffered no check by the Reformation: and we can only account for the vast number of Faust-like legends to this day current among the peasantry by supposing that, like the Puritans of old, they interpret literally the words of the apostle, which describe the enemy as " going about seeking whom he shall devour." As a specimen of this numerous class of our popular tales we give the following, often told as a warning against the deceitful practices with which Satan is apt to deceive the unwary :—

A farmer had once occasion to leave home for a week ; and previous to his going gave strict orders to one of his lads to spread a certain field with manure, already on the land in the customary heaps. Gaffer gone, the boy thought no more of the spreading, but made holiday all the week. On the day appointed for his master's return the young idler gave way to the fear of punishment, and lay on the ground bitterly bemoaning his situation. While thus employed he is accosted by a little old man, the form usually assumed by Lucifer on these predatory excursions. " What's the matter, my lad ?" quoth he. " I bent done me wurk, zur," sobbed the child. " Never mind," said the little man. " Canst run ?" " Eez, zur," was the reply. " Then off with ye to yonder stile, and if I do your work and catch you before you're there, *your mine.*" This speech informs the

lad of the real character of his visitor; but the fear of
temporal chastisement prevails over spiritual, and off
he goes. Instantly the soil begins to fly about in all
directions, and in a few minutes he sees his work done,
and his adversary coming after him at full speed. A
desperate neck-or-nothing "chivvy" is this same race
for a soul; but, as frequently happens in his encounters
with mortals, the "old un" is foiled, and the boy succeeds in leaping the stile just as he feels the burning
grasp of his adversary on his "smock." At night the
farmer returned, and, finding the work done, rewarded
the boy; but on the following morning the manure
was found collected again in the heaps, and the field
remained in its former state.

AGRICULTURAL FESTIVALS.

SHEEP-SHEARING.

THE operations of sheep-shearing, like those of harvest
and seed-time, were formerly wound up by a feast, at
which furmety and cheesecake formed the principal
delicacies. The meal is still sometimes given, but the
modern usage presents but a shadowy resemblance to
the ancient festivity, and has in many cases degenerated
into a large seed-cake, which it is customary to send to
the field, where it is eaten by the workmen on the scene
of their labours. Clare has prettily described the
modern customs peculiar to this festival :—

"Though fashion's haughty frown hath thrown aside
 Half the old forms simplicity supplied;
 Yet there are some pride's winter deigns to spare,
 Left like green ivy when the trees are bare.
 And now, when shearing of the flocks is done,
 Some ancient customs, mixed with harmless fun,
 Crown the swain's merry toils.   The timid maid,
 Pleased to be praised, and yet of praise afraid,
 Seeks the best flowers : not those of woods and fields,
 But such as every farmer's garden yields.

     *   *   *   *   *   *

 These the maid gathers with a coy delight,
 And ties them up in readiness for night :
 Then gives to ev'ry swain,'tween love and shame,
 Her "clipping posies," as his yearly claim.
 He rises to obtain the custom'd kiss :
 With stifled smiles, half hankering after bliss,
 She shrinks away, and blushing, calls it rude ;
 Yet turns to smile, and hopes to be pursued :
 While one, to whom the hint may be applied,
 Follows to gain it, and is not denied."

So far have we preserved a few of the old observances—

"But the old beechen bowl, that once supplied
 The feast of furmety, is thrown aside ;
 And the old freedom that was living then,
 When masters made them merry with their men ;
 When all their coats alike were russet brown,
 And his rude speech was vulgar as their own :—
 All this is past, and soon will pass away
 The time-torn relic of the holiday."

HARVEST-HOME.

It is customary to decorate the last or " harvest load"
with boughs of oak and ash, and the men, who all ride

home upon it, sing with stentorian voices some such
rude rhymes as the following, varying it slightly in
different districts :—

> "Harvest home! harvest hum!
> Harvest home!
> We've plough'd,
> We've sown,
> We've ripp'd,
> We've mown.
> Harvest home! harvest hum!
> We want water, and kaint get nun."

The waggon is pursued by young women bearing bowls
of water, and at the intimation conveyed in the last line
their contents are hurled upon the singers.* In some
parts of the county it is customary for the farmer to
send some of his men to ring the church bells; and
when this is the case the burden is varied to—

> " Harvest home! harvest home!
> The boughs they do shake, and the bells they do ring;
> So merrily we bring harvest in, harvest in ;
> So merrily we bring harvest in."

These ceremonies attendant upon the bringing home
of the last load form such an important item of the
harvest-home festivities that in many districts the

---

* This curious sprinkling custom still obtains in Buckinghamshire. " In September, 1787, an inquisition was taken at Weedon,
in the county of Bucks, on view of the body of William Clark, who,
as he was climbing into a tree, to throw water on some people who
were riding on a load of beans, called the harvest-home load, fell
from the same to the ground, broke one of his legs, and received
several internal bruises, of which he languished till the next day,
and then died."—*Northampton Mercury.*

N

epithet " cart" has been transferred from the veritable
vehicle to the feast itself.   Vide *Glossary* in *v.*

The harvest feast, or supper, is still retained in many
places, though rapidly disappearing before the modern
practice of giving the men money to spend at the
" public."   After a substantial meal of roast beef and
plum-pudding, the evening is passed in various games
and sports.   *Vide* CRANE, HOGS, &c. in *Glossary.*   Rude
farces form one of the most popular of these entertain-
ments.   We select a specimen (called the *Scotch Pedlars,
or the Scotchman's Pack*), given in the Introduction
to the *Village Minstrel*, and described in the poet's own
words :—" Two men come in covered with blankets,
stuffed with straw at their back.   They call out as
they come in, ' corks and blue,' and then sit down and
call for ale, the scene being a public-house.   They begin
to drink, and run over droll stories and recollections of
their former travels, &c.   One, seeming more covetous
of beer than the other (whose tongue keeps him employed), takes, every now and then, a pull at the
tankard, as opportunity offers, unknown to his talka-
tive companion, in consequence of which the tankard is
often empty and filled ; and on calling for the reckoning,
the other, who has been busied in discourse, starts,
surprised at the largeness of the bill, and refuses payment.   The other, nearly drunk, reels and staggers
about, and stubbornly resists all persuasions of satisfac-
tion on his part, which brings on a duel with their long
staves, driving each other out of the room as a termination to the scene."

In the northern parts of the county, where the

manner of observing the festival resembles more strongly
the East Anglian method, it is customary for the
labourers to beg "largess" from the tradesmen with
whom their master is in the habit of dealing.   The
money so obtained is spent in ale drinking.

EANING-TIDE.

In the southern district it is customary on the birth
of the first lamb to regale the shepherds with pancakes.

CUSTOMS ON PARTICULAR DAYS.

ST. VALENTINE'S DAY.

On this day it is the custom for children of both sexes
to go round to the doors of the principal houses in the
villages, singing—

> "Good morrow, Valentine;
> Plaze to give me a Valentine :
> I'l be yourn, if ye'l be mine :
> Good morrow, Valentine."

This is called "gwain valentinin," and they are
generally rewarded with pence or apples, which are
afterwards equally divided among them.

SHROVE-TIDE.

The old custom of throwing at cocks at this season,
formerly current throughout England, is now nearly, if

not quite, extinct. It was declining during the latter
part of the last century, as appears from the following
paragraph in the *Northampton Mercury* of February,
1788 :—" We cannot but express our wishes that
persons in power, as well as parents and masters of
families, would exert their authority in suppressing a
practice too common at this season—throwing at cocks,
a custom which, to the credit of a civilized people, is
annually declining." The custom of having pancakes
on Shrove Tuesday is still most religiously adhered to.

MAY-DAY.

In our feasts and popular festivals we still retain, in
a great measure, the old Julian calendar. To this
day, among the Northamptonshire hamlets, May-day is
reckoned to fall on the eleventh.

Maypoles, indeed, are rapidly becoming extinct; but
traces of the old festivity remain in the processions of
children which on this day perambulate our villages.
A " May lord" and " May lady" are chosen to rule the
revels; and these dignitaries, attended by a numerous
retinue of young girls, attired in white, and accompanied by an enormous garland, formed principally of
hawthorn blossom, proceed from door to door, begging
pence for the holiday. The money so obtained is spent
in feasting; and the games of the day are usually ter-
minated by a dance on the green. In some parts of the
county it is usual to leave a branch of May at each
house, with the following rhyming address, savouring
strongly of puritan adaptation :—

> " A branch of May I have brought you,
>   And at your door it stands :
>   Well set out, and well spread about,
>   By the work of our Lord's hands.
>   Take a Bible in your hands,
>   Read a chapter through ;
>   And when the day of judgment comes,
>   God will remember you.
>   God bless ye all, both *gret* and small,
>   And I wish ye a merry May."

Sometimes the address is varied to —

> " Arise ! arise ! ye dairy maids,
>   Shake off your drowsy dreams ;
>   Step straightway unto your dairies,
>   And fetch us a bowl of cream :
>   If not a bowl of your sweet cream,
>   A *tot* of your brown beer ;
>   And if we should stop to tarry in the town,
>   We'll come *agen* another year."

May-games and ceremonials appear to have received a terrible blow during the reign of fanaticism. Superstition, indeed, it did not banish; but it was the ruin of all our popular festivals—few have survived it, and those few have been so miserably shorn as scarcely to be recognised. In 1661, one Thomas Hall, B.D., and Pastor of King's Norton, in this county, fulminated against them in a book, which he entitled, "*Funebria Floræ, the Downfall of May-games;* wherein is set forth the rudeness, profaneness, &c., contempt of God and godly magistrates, ministers, and people, which oppose the rascality and rout in this their open prophanenesse and Heathenish customs, occasioned by the generall com-

plaint of the rudeness of people in this kind, in this
interval of settlement, &c. &c." It is, as the author
observes, " a kind of dialogue ; and dialogues have ever
been accounted the most lively and delightful, the most
facile and fruitfullest way of teaching."

The book contains a few local notices :—" There were
two May-poles set up in my parish : the one was stollen,
and the other was given by a professed papist. That
which was stollen was said to be given, when 'twas
proved to their faces that 'twas stollen ; and they were
made to acknowledge their offence. This pole that was
stollen was rated at 5s. : if all the poles, one with
another, were so rated which were stollen this way,
what a considerable summ would it amount to. . . . . .
Fighting and bloodshed is usual at such meetings, inasmuch that 'tis a common saying, that 'tis no festival
unless there be some fighting."   p. 10.

As it is probable that the worthy B.D. took his
examples from his own neighbourhood, we give the
following from the speech of the May-pole :—

> " I have a mighty retinue,
> The skimm of all the raskall crew,
> Of fidlers, pedlers, jaylescapt slaves ;
> Of tinkers, turncoats, tosspot knaves ;
> Of theeve and scape thrifts, many a one ;
> With bouncing Besse and dancing Jone ;
> With idle boys and journeymen,
> And vagrants that their country run :
> Yea ! hobby-horse does hither prance,
> Maid Marrian and the Morris dance.
> My summons fetcheth far and near,
> All that can swagger, roar, and swear ;

All that can dance, and drab, and drink,
They run to me as to a sink.
These mee for their commander take,
And I do them my blackguards make."

The puritanical doctrines of their pastor appear to
have been very distasteful to the Nortonians. "This
last May," says he, "opposing some Floralians in their
prophane practices (whom I thought after above twenty
years' preaching should have learnt better things), they
gave out that I was little better than a quaker, a
preacher of false doctrine, and an enemy to the king,
and should be thrown out of my place ; and why so—
because I hindered practical fanaticks in their frantic
practices."

TANDER.

The name given to the festival of St. Andrew, old
style, Dec. 11th, of which it is a corruption.

Of all the numerous red-letter days which diversified
the lives of our ancestors, this is the only one which
has survived to our own times in anything like its
pristine character. St. Andrew appears to be looked
upon by the lace-makers as their patron saint ; which
may perhaps account for the estimation in which his
festival is held. In many places, where progress has
not yet shown her face, the day is one of unbridled
licence—a kind of miniature carnival. Village "schol-
ards" bar out their master ; the lace-schools are deserted,
and drinking and feasting prevail to a riotous extent.
Towards evening the sober villagers appear to have
become suddenly smitten with a violent taste for mas-

querading. Women may be seen walking about in
male attire, while men and boys have donned the female
dress, and visit each other's cottages, drinking hot " eldern
wine," the staple beverage of the season.   Then commences the *Mumming*, too often described to need mention here, save to note that in the rude drama performed
in the Northamptonshire villages, St. George has given
place to George III., and the dragon, formerly the
greatest attraction of the piece, been supplanted by
Napoleon, who is annually killed on this night in personal encounter with the aforesaid monarch, to the
intense delight and edification of the loyal audience.
Notwithstanding the change in the dramatis personæ,
the rhymes are but slightly altered, and the legerdemain
tricks of the fool, the " travels of the egg," alluded to
by Ben Jonson, are still to be observed.   The speech
of King George, introducing the fiend, is remarkably
similar to the one given by Mr. Chambers as current in
the West of Scotland.   Vide *Popular Rhymes of Scotland*, p. 304.

> " Here comes old Belzebub,
> On his yead he kyars a club,
> In his hons he 's a drippin pon ;
> Dwant ye think he 's a jolly old mon ? "

The fool, who is also musician, introduces himself in
the following speech :—

> " Here comes I as is nar bin yit,
> Wi' my gret yead an little wit :
> My yead's too big, an my wit's too small,
> So I 'll play ye a tune to plaze ye all."

It is singular that these festivities, looked upon as commencing the joyous season of Christmas, and by no means confined to Northamptonshire, should have escaped the researches of all previous collectors.

CHRISTMAS.

Christmas-eve is well known to love-sick swains and languishing maidens as the day, above all others, most favourable for obtaining a glimpse into futurity. Numerous are the spells and ceremonies by which this is attempted. Among the most commonly practised are, baking the dumb cake (a divination also performed on the eve of St. Mark, *q. v.*), sowing hemp-seed, and eating the salt egg. At the " witching hour of midnight" on this eve, the young damsel who goes into the garden and plucks twelve sage-leaves, will see the shadowy form of her future husband approaching her from the opposite end of the ground. In trying this experiment great care must be taken not to break or damage the sage-stalk ; if this should happen, serious consequences would ensue. The following barbarous charm is also commonly used :—The heart is taken from a *living* pigeon, stuck full of pins, and laid on the hearth ; while burning, the form of the experimenter's future helpmate becomes visible to her eyes. Others, again, practise a divination in order to hear some sound significant of the trade of their husbands that are to be. A young damsel informed the compiler that while performing the requisite ceremony she heard, or fancied she heard, a sound like the falling of a bag of nails, and, therefore, ever after-

wards firmly believed that she was destined to become
the bride of a blacksmith.

Northamptonshire is not rich in carols : in many of
our villages the psalms have been substituted ; and the
strains of old Hopkins and Sternhold, when wafted by
the frosty breeze of a winter's evening, fall not un-
pleasantly upon the ears of the traveller. The singers
are usually regaled at each house with toast and ale,
and the money collected on such occasions is generally
expended in a dinner.

Christmas night is usually spent in merry-making,
and the yule block or clog is still offered up on the shrine
of old Father Christmas. When only half burnt it is
taken from the fire, and carefully preserved in the
cellar, or some other safe place, where it is not likely to
be disturbed, its possession being looked upon as bringing good luck to the house, and preventing fire throughout the coming year.

There is an old saying, still devoutly believed, that
if the sun makes his appearance on Christmas day (for
however short a time) the ensuing year will be a good
one for fruit.

It is still an article of popular belief that he who has
the courage to watch the cattle on Christmas-eve will
observe them, just as "the iron tongue of midnight
hath told twelve," to fall upon their knees, and hail
with devotion the anniversary of the Nativity. Rustics,
also, carefully avoid cross-roads on this eventful night,
as the ghosts of the unfortunate people buried there
have particular license to wander about, and wreak
their evil designs upon defenceless humanity.

ST. MARK'S EVE.

On St. Mark's eve it is still a custom about us for young maidens to make the *dumb cake*, a mystical ceremony, which has lost its origin, and in some counties may have ceased altogether. The number of the party never exceeds three: they meet in silence to make the cake, and as soon as the clock strikes twelve they each break a portion off to eat, and when done they walk up to bed backwards, without speaking a word, for if one speaks the spell is broken. Those that are to be married see the likeness of their sweethearts hurrying after them, as if wishing to catch them before they get into bed, but the maids, being apprized of this beforehand (by the caution of old women who have tried it), take care to unpin their clothes before they start, and are ready to slip into bed before they can be caught by the pursuing shadow; if nothing is seen, the desired token may be a knocking at the doors, or a rustling in the house as soon as they have retired. To be convinced that it comes from nothing else but the desired cause, they are always particular in turning out the cats and dogs before the ceremony begins. Those that are to die unmarried neither see nor hear anything; but they have terrible dreams, which are sure to be of new-made graves, winding-sheets, and church-yards, and of rings that will fit no finger, or which, if they do, crumble into dust as soon as put on. There is another dumb ceremony, of eating the yolk of an egg in silence, and then filling the shell with salt, when the

sweetheart is sure to make his visit in some way or
other before morning.   On the same night, too, the
more stout-hearted watch the church porch : they go
in the evening and lay in the church porch a branch of
a tree or a flower, large enough to be readily found in
the dark, and then return home to wait the approach
of midnight.   They are to proceed to the porch again
before the clock strikes twelve, and to remain in it till
it has struck ; as many as choose accompany the maid
who took the flower or branch, and is to fetch it again,
as far as the church gate, and there wait till their
adventuring companion returns, who, if she is to be
married within the year, is to see a marriage procession
pass by her, with a bride in her own likeness hanging
upon the arm of her future husband : as many brides-
men and maidens as appear to follow them, so many
months is the maid to wait before her marriage.

If she is to die unmarried, then the expected procession is to be a funeral, consisting of a coffin covered
with a white sheet, borne on the shoulders of shadows
that seem without heads.   This custom, with all its
contingent " hopes and fears," is still practised, though
with what success I am not able to determine.   The
imagination may be wrought to any height in such
matters, and, doubtless, some persuade themselves that
they see what the story describes.   An odd character
at Helpstone, whose name is Ben Barr, and whom the
villagers call and believe as " the prophet," watches the
church porch every year, and pretends to know the
fate of every one in the villages round, and who shall

be married or die in the year ; but as a few pence generally purchase a good omen, he seldom prophesies the death of his believers.*

EASTER SUNDAY.

The person who dons no new article of wearing apparel on this day will be unlucky throughout the year.

Rain on Easter day presages badly for the hay-crop ; hence the proverb—

" Rain on Easter-day,
Plenty of grass, but little good hay."

GOOD FRIDAY.

He who bakes or brews on Good Friday will have his house burnt down before the end of the year.

LENT.

To marry in Lent is extremely unlucky—Ash Wednesday particularly so.

* Communicated to Hone's Every-day Book, vol. i. p. 523-4, by a correspondent near Peterborough, signing himself ¶ ¶.

NORTHAMPTONSHIRE PROVERBS.

———

"IF WE CAN PADWELL OVERGOE, AND HORESTONE WE
    CAN SEE,
THEN LORDS OF ENGLAND WE SHALL BE."

"That there was a battle at Danesmore, betwixt the
Saxons and the Danes, the name of the place, and constant
tradition of the inhabitants, may reasonably incline us to
believe.   The people there have a notable rhime, which they
make the Danes to say upon the point of battel.   Padwell
is a noted flush spring in Edgcote grounds.   Horestone, a
       old stone upon the borders of Warwickshire (in
Wardlington field)."—*Morton.*

" WANSFORD, IN ENGLAND."

" Another, though less tragical, instance of the greatness
and suddeness of the inundations of the Nyne, is that well
known and not unpleasant story of a man who, as he was
fast asleep on a little haycock in a meadow on the Nyne, nigh
Wansford, never dreaming either of floods or rain, was
carry'd off by one of these floods, with his haycock under
him.   The poor man at length awakes, and looks about him
with all the surprise imaginable.   He had laid down to sleep
on a haycock in a dry meadow nigh Wansford, but finds
himself afloat in the midst of waters, for ought he knew, in
the wide ocean ; and, as the story goes, one espying him in
this condition, calls to him, and enquires where he lived.
The poor fellow, in a piteous tone, reply'd, ' At Wansford, in
England.'   However, the memory of the accident is preserved in the sign of the chief inn at Wansford.   And thence

the common proverbial saying of, living at Wansford, in England ; so common hereabouts that I admire it escaped Mr. Fuller, in his collection of *Local Proverbs*."—*Morton.*

" THE MAYOR OF NORTHAMPTON OPENS OYSTERS WITH HIS DAGGER."

To keep them at a sufficient distance from his nose.

" This town being 80 miles from the sea, sea-fish may be presumed stale therein. Yet have I heard that oysters (put up with care, and carried in the cool) were weekly brought fresh and good to Althorpe, the house of Lord Spencer, at equal distance."—*Fuller.*

" HE THAT MUST EAT A BUTTERED FAGGOT LET HIM GO TO NORTHAMPTON."

" Because it is the dearest town in England for fuel, where no coles can come by water, and little wood doth grow on land. Camden saith of this county in general, that it is, ' Silvis nisi in ulteriori et citeriori parte, minus lætus.' And if so when he wrote fifty years since, surely it is less woody in our age."— *Fuller.*

To which adds *Grose*—

" This was formerly the case, but the river Nen having many years ago been made navigable, coal-barges come up to the town, so that fuel is now to be bought at a very reasonable price."

" BRACKLEY BREED, BETTER TO HANG THAN TO FEED."

" Brackley is a decayed market-town and borough, which, abounding with poor, and troubling the country about with beggars, came into disgrace with its neighbours. I hear now that this place is grown industrious and thriving, and endeavours to wipe off this scandal."—*Ray.*

"SLAPTON,
        WHERE FOOLS WILL HAPPEN."

Slapton is a village near Towcester, and the above rhyme is often used to excite the irascibility of its inhabitants.—*Oral.*

"NASEBY CHILDREN."

Naseby children is a term proverbially applied to the aged here, from the frequent instances of their surviving the mental powers. Mastin records that one Corby, of this place, who died at the advanced age of 94, cut an entire new and regular set of teeth after he had attained his 70th year.

A Northamptonshire "*Blazon*" is also given in Drayton's *Poly-Olbion*, part ii. p. 71. Lond. 1622.

NOTES TO FAIRY SUPERSTITIONS.

A.

So, also, in the Danish and German legends, the person who beheld the elves through a knot-hole became immediately blind. *See* Mr. Croker's excellent translation of Grimm, *On the Nature of the Elves. Fairy Legends and Traditions of the South of Ireland*, part iii. p. 116.

In "the trickes of the women fayries," described in the curious black-letter tract, published at London in 1628, under the title of *Robin Goodfellow; his Mad Prankes and Merry Jests*, reprinted in Mr. Halliwell's *Illustrations of the Fairy Mythology of a Midsummer Night's Dream*, occurs the following :—" To walke nightly, as the men fayries we use not ; but now and then we go together, and at good huswives fire we warme and dresse our fayry children. If wee find cleane water and cleane towels, wee leave them money, either in their basons or in their shooes; but if wee find no clean water in their houses we wash our children in their pottage, milke, or beere, or what-ere we find."

The Craven "*dobbies*" resemble the Northamptonshire fairies in the custom of visiting the cottage hearth. "Some of the dobbies are contented to stay in outhouses with the cattle, but others will only dwell among human beings. The latter are thought to be fond of heat, but when the hearth cools it is said they frisk and racket about the house, greatly disturbing the inmates."—*Willan's Collection of West Riding Words*, Archæologia, vol. xvii.

B.

An Hampshire legend very similar is given in No. 430 of the *Literary Gazette*. The Northamptonshire tale limits the depredators to two, but the more Southern legend substitutes a whole fairy community.

The love of milk was an attribute of all the fairy-folk. Hobbes, in the amusing parallel which he draws between the Papacy and the "Kingdome of Fairies," gives the passage, never before, we believe, quoted, on this curious subject :— " The ecclesiastiques take the cream of the land by donations of ignorant men, that stand in awe of them, and by tythes : so, also, it is in the fable of the fairies, that they enter into the dairies, and feast upon the cream, which they skim from the milk." One of Puck's favourite pranks was to—

> " Skim milk, and sometimes labour in the quern,
> And bootless make the breathless housewife churn."

So, also, Randolf, who has made great use of these tiny beings in his dramas :—

> " I know no haunts, I have but to the dairy,
> To skim the milk-bowls, like a lickorish fairy."

C.

This legend is highly curious, as exhibiting the connexion of elves with trees. The elf evidently resided in the oak, and naturally pleaded for the safety of his dwelling.

Grimm gives many instances of this connexion. Certain trees were consecrated to their resort in Denmark. Elberich is represented as lying under a lime tree ; and among the ancient Prussians the elder was sacred to him, a superstition also still obtaining in Denmark. *Vide* Thiele's *Folke-sagn*, vol. i. p. 132 It was also the custom in Germany to pay particular respect to this tree on the first of May, or about Midsummer, when the elves, if light, are said to go in procession. Destroying the trees particularly raises the ire of the Scandinavian elves. A farmer felling trees, and squaring timber in the forest, vexed the mountain spirit, which asked, in a lamentable tone, " Who is making so much noise here !" " A Christian," replied his fellow, " has come here, and hews down the wood of our favourite haunts, and does us much injury." In Norway, too, certain high trees are forbidden, on their account, to be cut down.

Our elves were noted for their craft and cunning. The Devonshire legend of the "*Fox and the three Pixies*," which appeared some time since in the Folk-lore columns of the *Athenæum*, is well known in the Southern parts of Northamptonshire. In one of our versions of it a giant takes the place of the fox, who is tricked by the elf in the same manner.

The unreal and illusive nature of fairy gifts is also one of the characteristics of the Welsh elves. "It is related in Breconshire that fairies were accustomed to be seen by those who had the courage to look in the meadows, and often, 'when in sportive mood,' would present to the peasantry what appeared loaves of bread, but when examined in the morning were found to be toad-stools."— *Howell's Cambrian Superstitions*, Tipton, 1831, p. 146. In an Highland legend given by Stewart (*Popular Superstitions of Scotland*, p. 130), the elves substitute an unreal animal for the veritable cow, which has been abstracted by them.

D.

A similar tradition attaches itself to the origin of many other buildings throughout Great Britain. Mr. Chambers, in his *Popular Rhymes*, records many instances of its occurrence in Scotland; and in England we may point out the church of Bughton, in Sussex; Ambrosden Church, in Buckinghamshire; and that of Rochdale, in Yorkshire. Similar legends are also related of the churches of Great Brington and Oxendon, in this county, both of which, it is said, were originally intended to have been built on sites some distance from the present edifices.

Baker assigns a more matter-of-fact origin for the appellation "Nine Churches." "Stowe," he says, "received its adjunct of 'Nine Churches' because there was nine advowsons appendant to the manor."

The form of the hog was one of Puck's numerous disguises: thus in the *Midsummer Night's Dream*, act iii. sc. 1 :—

> " Sometimes a horse I'll be, sometimes a hound,
> A hog, a headless bear, sometimes a fire."

So, also, in *Robin Goodfellow ; his Mad Prankes and Merry Jests,* reprinted by the Percy Society :—

> " Thou has the power to change thy shape,
> To horse, to *hog,* to dog, to ape."

E.

The first part of this tale runs almost word for word with the Danish legend given by Thiele, " *How a Farmer tricks a Troll ;*" and the Story of Rabelais, " *How a Junior Devil was fooled by a Husbandman of Pope Figland*" (*Works,* ed. 1807, vol. iii. p. 291), but the incident of the mowing is wanting in both.

The curious proverb at page 138, which at once introduces us to the principal personages of Northamptonshire mythology, will remind the reader of the German one recorded by Grimm, " *To laugh like a Kobold ;*" or the Norfolk one, preserved by Forby, " *To laugh like Robin Goodfellow,*" spoken of a hearty horse laugh.

F.

The Northamptonshire legend runs thus :—Two brothers are reduced by the badness of the times to seek shelter in a hut built in the midst of a forest, where they subsist upon the juicy haunches of the king's deer. It appears that the same scarcity which drove the hunters to the woods affected also, in a similar way, the fairy denizens of the neighbouring wastes. One day, whilst the eldest brother remains behind to cook the meat, there enters a little Redman, with the modest request, " Plase gie me a few broth." Up the ladder rushes the hunter to find the hatchet, intending to inflict summary vengeance upon the intruder; but in the mean time the little Redman seizes the pot from the fire, and makes off. The exasperated cook pursues, but soon loses the cunning fiend among the intricacies of the forest. After a similar adventure, befalling the other brother on the following day, it becomes the turn of the much-despised youngest to prepare the meal for the absent brethren. Profiting by the mishaps of his comrades, and well knowing that a caught Redman, like the Cluricaune, proved a treasure to his captor, he lies in wait for his visitor behind the door ; and no sooner has the unsuspecting spirit entered, and given utterance to his usual phrase, " Plaze gie me a few broth," than he finds himself a prisoner. After many fruitless endeavours to escape, he conducts his captor to his residence—an old well, in a retired part of the forest ; and there ransoms himself with such store of gold, that his vanquisher, to quote, my narrator, " is made a mon on for life."

It is almost unnecessary to point out the affinity of this sprite with the Scottish *Redcap*, and the Irish *Fir Darrig*, of which latter his designation is a literal translation.

The following reached the compiler while the foregoing sheets were passing through the press :—

PEACOCK'S FEATHER.—Having a peacock's feather in the house is considered a bad omen,—many considering that sickness is surely the result.

HIRING A SERVANT.—If the money given as earnest is handed to the servant on the stairs, it is believed that she will not remain to fulfil her engagement. In such a case it will be thought advisable to recall her, and by some excuse obtain the money back again, and afterwards present it to her in a more suitable place.

WISHING-BONE.—The person to whose share falls the merry-thought of a fowl (in Northamptonshire called a wishing-bone), should immediately wish, and if within the bounds of possibility it will come to pass.

LIST OF ABBREVIATIONS.

Ak.	Akerman's Wiltshire Glossary.
A. S.	Anglo Saxon.
B. and F. . .	Beaumont and Fletcher.
Bar.	Barnes' Glossary of Dorsetshire Words.
Bat.	Batchelor's List of Bedfordshire Words, appended to the Orthoepical Analysis of the English Language.
Broc.	Brockett's North Country Words, ed. 1829.
Belg.	Belgic.
C.	Canting Dictionary (see p. 21).
Car.	Carr's Craven Dialect, ed. 1824.
Clare	The Glossaries to the Village Minstrel and Poems illustrative of Rural Life and Scenery, of John Clare.
Dan.	Danish.
Dut.	Dutch.
Ev.	Evans' Leicestershire Words, Phrases, and Proverbs.
Ex.	Glossary to the Exmoor Dialogue.
For.	Forby's East Anglian Vocabulary, 1830.
Fr.	French.
Gael.	Gaelic.
Germ.	German.
Goth.	Gothic.
Hart.	Hartshorne's Shropshire Glossary, appended to his Salopia Antiqua.
Her.	Herefordshire Glossary, 1839.
Hunt.	Hunter's Hallamshire Glossary.
Ic.	Icelandic.
It.	Italian.

Jam.	Jamieson's Dictionary of the Scottish Language.
Jen.	Jennings' Somersetshire Glossary, 1825.
Lanc. . . .	Glossary at the end of Tim Bobbin's Lancashire Dialect.
M.	Marshall's Rural Economy of the Midland Counties. Glossary, at pp. 377-389, vol. ii.
M. Yorks. . .	Marshall's Glossary to the Rural Economy of Yorkshire.
Moor	Moor's Suffolk Words and Phrases, 1823.
Morton . . .	Natural History of Northamptonshire, 1712.
n.	North.
Pal.	Palmer's Glossary of the Devonshire Dialect.
part.	Participle.
pron.	Pronounced.
pret.	Preterite.
s.	The south-western dialect.
Shaks. . . .	Shakespeare.
Sp.	Spanish.
Sw.	Swedish.
Sui-G. . . .	Sui-Gothic.
Tees.	Teesdale Glossary. Lond. 1849.
Teut.	Teutonic.
Wel.	Welsh.
Wilb.	Wilbraham's Cheshire Glossary, 1826.
Wil.	Willan's Ancient Words of the West Riding of Yorkshire, communicated to vol. xviii. of the Archæologia, published by the Society of Antiquaries.

THE END.

Printed by J. Rickerby, 15, Sherbourn Lane, King William Street, City.

Lightning Source UK Ltd.
Milton Keynes UK
UKHW020015100223
416721UK00002B/460